FIVE
SEASONS
OF JAM

LILLIE O'BRIEN
OF LONDON BOROUGH OF JAM

photography by Elena Heatherwick
Kyle Books

An Hachette UK Company
www.hachette.co.uk

First published in Great Britain in 2018
by Kyle Books, an imprint of Kyle Cathie Ltd
Carmelite House, 50 Victoria Embankment
London EC4Y 0DZ
www.kylebooks.co.uk

ISBN 978 0 85783 439 3

Distributed in the US by Hachette Book Group,
1290 Avenue of the Americas, 4th and 5th Floors,
New York, NY 10104

Distributed in Canada by Canadian Manda Group, 664
Annette St., Toronto, Ontario, Canada M6S 2C8

Designer: Marcus Haslam
Photographer: Elena Heatherwick
Props Stylist: Alix McAlister
Project Editor: Sophie Allen
Editorial Assistant: Sarah Kyle
Production: Nic Jones, Gemma John and Lisa Pinnell

A Cataloguing in Publication record for this title is
available from the British Library.

Printed and bound in China

10 9 8 7 6 5 4 3 2

CONTENTS

My fascination with jam and preserving started when I was growing up in Melbourne, Australia. We grew our own produce at home and I used to help my mum make preserves with the gluts of fruit and vegetables: tomatoes, figs, lemons and basil – all ingredients that like the heat. I was so excited by the process of trapping flavours and colours in a jar that would then sit untouched for as long as two years before we would twist off the lid and immediately be transported back to their spirit. I love vividly coloured fruit – the brighter the better – they really inspire me when looking for new flavour combinations – capturing that vibrancy in a jar is exciting.

My early experiences of preserving memories and stories in jars were the inspiration for my career in food, leading me by way of several restaurant kitchens to the other side of the world and all the way back to jam.

It wasn't until 2008, when I started working as a pastry chef at St. John Bread and Wine in London, that I had the chance to revisit my early love of picking and preserving. During my time in the kitchen I really discovered seasonal produce in the UK, and how to preserve the essence of a season while a fruit is fleetingly available. 'Seasonality' is more defined here in the UK than back home in Australia due to the latitude. At St. John, we would make orange marmalade in January, coinciding with the short season of the bitter oranges grown around Seville – enough to last the year. Moving into the summer months, we would buy as much tasty overripe fruit as we could to bottle and make jams for the colder months. The cooking ethos at St. John is not only to use everything from 'nose to tail' but also to respect seasonality. I had never before worked in a restaurant that honoured ingredients like this. It was really exciting to celebrate produce when it was in its prime. If strawberries tasted amazing we would just serve them in a bowl completely untouched – why would you want to do anything to something that was so naturally delicious?

Preserving was also a huge part of the pastry kitchen because we had such limited supplies in winter; after a while, even chocolate, lemons and apples could become a bit gloomy. It was crucial for us to be able to bottle the brightness and optimism of spring, summer and autumn to serve in the restaurant during those darker months. Our local fruit and vegetable supplier would telephone us during the peak fruiting season, offering us what he had found in abundance at the market that night; any fruit that was too juicy or the ones discarded for not being the right colour, shape or size – we wanted them.

I started making my own jams at home as a bit of a hobby, initially. The natural confidence I had gained working as a chef in restaurant kitchens helped me to develop new ideas, experimenting with different flavours, and adding flowers or spices to the jams to enhance the fruit. It was a time of huge freedom and fun for me.

Then, in 2011, I started running a stall at my local market every second Sunday to test out the jams I was making at home on real customers, rather than friends and family. The feedback I got was amazing – everyone seemed to love what I was doing, and this gave me the motivation to leave my job and try making jam full-time. I never really thought about it at the time but thinking back it was a crazy and bold move. In late 2012, I found a small retail space in the adjacent street to my house in Hackney and I turned it into a little jam shop and storeroom. To this day, I think London Borough of Jam (LBJ) is still London's only jam shop. I sell a lot of my jam wholesale and open the shop on weekends, where I like to test out new ideas on my loyal regular customers.

JAM AS MEDITATION

Something that I have learned and would love to pass on to my readers is that jam cannot be rushed. Jam recipes might seem short on the page, but they're designed to stretch time – from when you first create an idea for a new flavour combination to when you pop the lid off the jar as long as two years later and spread it on your toast.

In this book, I have created recipes to be lingered over, ones that inspire and give confidence to be a little more adventurous in the preserving kitchen. There is true spiritual pleasure to be had from jam. It isn't just a twee or fusty undertaking – for me, jam is all about exploration, discovery and harmony.

Jam and preserves don't usually have many ingredients so one of my main occupations is taking the time to gather ingredients and connect with the outdoors. I love the fact that I can go out into my garden, see what is growing and use whatever is in abundance. I hope this book will encourage you to get outdoors and start discovering what is around you, making the natural connection between the ingredients that grow together at the same time of year, responding to nature and working with the seasons.

JAM & TRAVEL

I love taking a few pots of jam home with me to Australia for my family to eat during the year, as I know it will remind them of me when spread on toast, or savoured by the teaspoonful. I like nothing better than when a customer tells me that they will be taking my jam to the other side of the world, too. Travel is a big part of LBJ and finding new fruit and flavours that might represent a new culture is really exciting for me. Every year we go to the same place in Greece and I love picking fresh figs from the front of the house and wild fennel pollen to make small batches of jam while we are there. You can't beat the quality of fresh fruit picked straight from a tree or shrub and placed almost instantly in a pan. One of the first things I like to do in a new country is go directly to the local market or supermarket and have a look around, picking up edibles that I have never seen before. Sometimes the best places will be right there on the roadside, like the service stations on the autostrada in Italy. Not only can you buy the most beautiful fresh produce in such places, but also amazing preserves, honey, herbs, oils and wines – all the good things associated with this food-focused country. A spirit of adventure and discovery is something that I would love you to take from these recipes, so be playful.

JAM AS HERITAGE

I can't think of many cultures that don't have a tradition of making preserves. Jam has a very long pedigree, dating back to first-century Rome. And throughout history jam has always been democratic: food for the people, not just the preserve of the few. Ordinary folk foraged for fruit and learned to store it to enrich their meagre diets, and jams with their keeping qualities proved an easy way of nourishing great armies on the move.

There are some strong traditions of preserving passed down the generations. It seems to me that the many benefits of preserving, like many other time-honoured techniques, such as fermenting, microbrewing, sourdough baking, have been rediscovered, at least here in the UK. Younger people today are embracing artisanal trades and are unafraid of experimenting, which is wonderful. Jam-making is a timeless craft. East London, where I live, is rich in cultural diversity and I'm lucky enough to be exposed to many palates and traditions, so many of which I love to playfully reflect in my jams.

THE FIVE SEASONS OF THE LBJ KITCHEN

It's lovely to capture a moment in time when you are making jam, as if to preserve a story by stirring it into the pot. That's why it's rewarding to seek out something special, a combination that's entirely seasonal and out of the ordinary, and make a moment of it. There's such excitement and adventure in going to pick more unusual fruit from a pick-your-own-farm, and such delicious suspense in waiting for your favourite fruit to come into season. Seasonality is really key: much as I love figs, I suspect that if we had them all year round, I wouldn't be as enamoured. I know when I make Fig & Earl Grey Jam (see page 100) every September everyone goes crazy for it – and that's because we all savour what we've been waiting for.

My jam-making year rotates around five seasons, each of which is a chapter in this book. This is a natural progression that came about simply by how I work every year, beginning in April:

ALIVE/ MID TO LATE SPRING
A season of blossoming florals and awakening

HOT/ SUMMER
A season of vivid sweetness

BLUSH/ EARLY AUTUMN
A time of smoky warmth and rich spice

BARB/ LATE AUTUMN
Days that are crisp and clear, with nature all thorns and spikes

FROST/ WINTER TO EARLY SPRING
The biting, the dark and the cosy

JAM-MAKING PRINCIPLES

STERILISATION

Efficient sterilisation is the key to successful jam-making. You need to ensure that you eliminate all food-spoiling yeasts and moulds that are present in your ingredients and in the jars that you will fill. Fruit that is cooked with sugar to the correct temperature and clean glass jars that have been heated to 110°C are going to preserve your jam for at least 12 months.

To sterilise your jars, wash them in warm soapy water and rinse thoroughly. Place them, open-side up, on a baking tray and put in an oven preheated to 110°C/225°F/gas mark ¼ and leave for 30 minutes. To sterilise lids, clips or rubber seals put a pan of water, bring to the boil and boil for 5 minutes, then turn off the heat and leave to rest.

I advise you to begin the sterilisation process when setting point (see below) is reached. You can always turn your oven off and leave the jars resting in the warm oven before using them – just don't allow them to become cold. Hot jam should always go into warm jars and be sealed with warm lids so that a seal is formed inside as the warmth pushes the air out. You can also turn your jars upside down to help push out the air but be careful with high-pectin fruit as they will set quickly and you'll have levitating jam.

SETTING POINT

Getting jam to set can seem tricky but usually you will only have problems if you haven't cooked the preserve for long enough or haven't added enough sugar. There are a few simple ways of testing the setting point. First, the good old-fashioned plate-in-the-freezer test. Place a ceramic saucer in the freezer overnight and the next day, when you want to test for setting point, place a teaspoonful of the jam on the frozen plate and run your index finger through it to see if it holds and has created a 'skin'. If it has, then you're good to go. The other way, which is a little more efficient, is by using a sugar thermometer and taking the boiling jam to 105°C/220°F. This is the setting point. Sometimes if I know the fruit is extremely high in pectin I may take it a little lower. For example, green gooseberries will set at 90°C/194°F, but generally speaking, 105°C/220°F is the rule. If you find that you haven't cooked your jam long enough and it hasn't set properly then recook it back into another fresh batch of jam. I don't like to reboil unset jam, though, as it ends up tasting like caramelised sugar – steer away from this.

Jellies can be tested the same but it is easier to see by eye. A good indication that it is ready is if you stir the boiling liquid with a wooden spoon and find that the bubbles rise up and look as if they will overflow, the top appearing almost foam-like. Jellies should also be heated to 105°C/220°F and correct pectin, acid and sugar levels will enable a good set.

STORAGE

The recipes in this book will, generally speaking, have a 12-month shelf life if stored in a cool dark place. Once open you can keep the jar refrigerated and take out a few hours before eating the preserve so that it isn't fridge cold.

FRUIT & WATER EVAPORATION

For me, the hardest thing about making preserves is getting them to set. I don't add any commercial pectin to my jams, which rely entirely on the natural pectin in the fruit, so while some may set easily others may need some experimentation. I have learnt throughout my jam-making years to tell this by the shape of the bubbles when the jam is boiling – an indication of how much of the fruit's natural water has evaporated. The water will evaporate but the sugar won't, so once the bubbles become more uniform in size (smaller) it's a good sign that it is about to set before becoming a caramel. Since sugar doesn't evaporate it is a good idea to ensure your jams are made with at least 25 per cent less sugar to fruit at the start of the boiling process; the proportions will equal out once the cooking process has finished. Most recipes call for equal amounts of fruit to sugar, which I don't understand as you will end up with a jam that contains more sugar than fruit, whereas it is perfectly possible to create fruit-driven jams with less sugar.

TOP TIPS FOR MAKING SMALL-BATCH JAM

- Ensure your jam pan is only half full of ingredients and no more – otherwise you risk the boiling contents overflowing.
- Use a wide pan, large enough to allow maximum evaporation of liquids in the quickest time possible. All recipes in this book have been cooked in a Mauviel 36cm/14in jam pan.
- Choose unblemished ripe fruit that taste good.
- Cooking times are a rough guide and will vary slightly.
- Don't cook more than 2kg fruit at a time.
- The quicker the cooking time, the better.
- Don't use hard unripe fruit because it won't break down.

MUST-HAVE EQUIPMENT IN THE LBJ KITCHEN

- Copper preserving pan (minimum 2kg weight) or heavy-based saucepan (stainless steel or cast iron)
- Heat-resistant spatula
- Microplane zester
- Jam funnel with a large hole for easy pouring
- Long-handled wooden spoon
- Electric scales
- Thermometer
- Cheesecloth/Muslin
- Mouli
- Ladle
- Large jug with good spout for pouring control
- Jars and bottles with lids

FRIENDS OF JAM

Leaves
Bay leaves
Blackcurrant leaves
Cherry leaves
Fig leaves
Grape leaves
Kaffir lime leaves
Oak leaves
Peach leaves
Scented geranium
  leaves

Kernels*
Apricot kernels
Cherry kernels
Nectarine kernels
Peach kernels
Plum kernels

Teas
Assam tea
Ceylon tea
Darjeeling tea
Earl Grey tea
Jasmine tea
Oolong tea

Spices
Cardamom
  (black and green)
Cinnamon
Juniper
Peppercorns
Saffron
Star anise
Vanilla

Wines & Spirits
Bourbon
Calvados
Eau de vie
Fino sherry
Grappa
Infused gin
Infused vodka
Kirsch
Marsala wine
Pernod
Sherry
Verjuice
Vermouth
Whiskey

Flowers & Herbs
Angelica
Chamomile
Cherry blossom

Dandelions
Dill flowers
Elderflowers
Flowering thyme
Gorse
Hibiscus
Lavender
Lemon balm
Lemon verbena
Lovage
Pineapple sage
Scented geraniums
Sweet cicely
Sweet woodruff
Tarragon
White sage
Wild fennel

* All kernels within the fruit stone contain small amounts of cyanide so eating large quantities is not advised. Once cooked out in a boiling jam these are safe but if in doubt please don't consume.

FLORAL

BLOSSOMY

AWAKENING

ITCHY

SNEEZY

A L

BROGDALE
FARM

After nearly 12 years of living in the UK, spring is now my favourite season. The long winter has come to an end and the earth is coming back to life. It's a time of awakening and excitement as we can look forward to longer, brighter days, the smell of narcissus and the explosions of blossom. It's also a time when there isn't an abundance of fruit. As I wait for the first of the strawberries at the start of May traditionally in southeast England (although often earlier due to the use of hot houses), I also begin to prepare syrups, cordials and pickles to have for the coming months – not only to flavour my jams but also in a bid to capture the spring that has just sprung.

Cherry blossom is one of those special flowers that, to me, is the essence of spring. In 2005 I lived in Japan for a year and since then I have an undeniable excitement for the delicate tissue paper-like flowers that explode with colour, creating a magical, if fleeting, display. The delicate blooms sometimes last just a few days at their peak before being swept off the trees by fierce winds or dashed to the ground by heavy rain. Catching them can be tricky – as I write this in mid-April, the cherry blossom has nearly finished here in London, while last year it was only just beginning.

In a bid to do some real research, I decided to visit the Brogdale Collections in Faversham, Kent, home to the National Fruit Collection. I wanted to see the different types of blossoms the trees were producing and try to gain a better understanding of the varieties I was picking from trees where I live in London. How did I know which species I was picking blossom from? How could I identify them? I wanted to understand what flavours I could get from each variety.

I arrived at the Brogdale Collections on a chilly, grey April day and was greeted by Mike Roser, my trusty tour guide. I quickly made it clear I was in search of cherry blossom and he told me that a sharp frost the week before meant that only a few flowers remained on the trees. I was disappointed that Mother Nature had swept past but I had to go with it. Instead, Mike showed me the apple trees in the original 45-year-old orchard, some of which were just starting to flower and were a delicate pink, while others were at their peak with pure white blossom and sweetly scented.

'Looking out over the vast orchard was overwhelming and trying to identify the different varieties seemed impossible.'

Mike explained that the apple collection held 2,500 varieties with two trees of each variety. Years earlier they had planted a new collection using the same 2,500 varieties of apple trees, which has now doubled the size of the orchard. Looking out over the vast orchard was overwhelming and trying to identify the different varieties seemed impossible. Thankfully, the cultivar signs on the trees made it clear and especially entertaining as I joked with Mike about the weird and wonderful names (Altländer Pfannkuchenapfel , Ballyfatten, Channel Beauty, Court Pendu Plat, Bloody Ploughman, Ellison's Orange and Kidd's Orange Red). Some of the blossoms had just started and were a pale pink colour while other more advanced blooms had faded to pure white as the flowering had progressed. There was a sweet smell from the flowers, which I imagined would become fragrant apples once the fruit started to grow.

Through the cyprus hedging, we moved on to the quince trees, elegantly shaped like giant umbrellas. All the quince appeared to be in full bloom, their flowers a pale, peachy pink, and looked much bushier and more robust than the apple trees, which are pruned over the years to be only a few metres tall. Come autumn, the 19 varieties of quince in this orchard will all yield yellow, knobbly, scented fruit, ready to be slow-cooked and passed through cheesecloth to make a ruby-red jelly.

I was keen to ask Mike about japonica as a former work colleague had given me over 10kg of fruit the previous year and I wanted to know the difference between the japonica and quince species, apart from the fact the japonica were much smaller. Flowering quince, or japonica, Mike explained, is a cultivar from China and Japan, whereas the quince tree originates from Western Asia. Japonica is a popular spring-flowering garden shrub that has red, white or pink flowers and bears very small fruit, usually with some red spots and blush on the skin, that make a superior jelly.

The final stop on our blossom tour was the cherry orchard. The trees were still holding on to the last of their delicate white flowers, a little bruised from the frost the week before. Because half of the trees were looking a little bare, I could see through the whole orchard and the ground beneath the trees. My eye was caught by numerous colourful rectangular boxes in the middle of the rows, which appeared to be literally buzzing with activity. Upon closer inspection, I discovered the boxes were full of bees that are placed in the orchard each spring, a practice used with all the fruit trees at Brogdale Collections to ensure the flowers are pollinated. Mike was especially keen to keep me away from the boxes in fear of me getting stung but I was instantly drawn to them as they were such a wonderful contrast to the trees, which were almost bare, reminding us of what great fruit were yet to come.

The cherry tree collection contains 285 varieties that have come from all over Europe and North America. The cherries are classed as red, white and black, based on the colour of their juice, although the fruit themselves range from yellow, creamy yellow, orange, bright red, and dark red. The trees with edible cherries are generally cultivars of *Prunus avium,* the wild sweet cherry, and *Prunus cerasus,* a sour cherry, both of which are different from the more common ornamental variety. *Prunus serrulata,* the Japanese flowering cherry, has more dramatic pink flowers and barely any fruit, making these trees a popular choice in parks and cities. It's the blossom from these trees that I generally pick for syrups and salting. The strong bitter marzipan flavour that the flowers produce is reminiscent of the the almond-flavoured kernel found in the stone.

As Brogdale is a national collection and part of an international programme to protect plant genetic resources, it is forbidden to pick anything in the orchards. Nothing goes to waste though and all the fruit harvested in summer and autumn is either used to make preserves to sell in their farm shop or kept for research purposes.

When you pick blossom from trees in your local area or, if you're lucky enough, your own garden, do be mindful that you are picking the fruit before it develops, so please don't take too much — consider the birds and bees. On my return to London I tried using different varieties of apple blossom to see the difference in flavour. I was lucky enough to be given a small amount of medlar blossom and crab apple blossom to experiment with. Cooked into a sugar syrup these flowers had a more subtle flavour than the cherry blossom.

The season for picking blossom is a short one and I try to be creative with my precious (treasured) harvest, making syrups and also dehydrating the flowers (see Salted Cherry Blossom, page 20). Preserved this way the flowers can be later used as decoration, ground into powders, immersed in sugars as a flavouring, salted and even steeped into custards and ice-cream bases. Try using lilac flowers, sweet cicely, sage, violets, wild garlic flowers or gorse flowers.

SALTED CHERRY BLOSSOM
Makes 1 x 300ml jar

In Japan, salted cherry blossom is used to mark special occasions, especially weddings and birthdays. Warm sakurayu (cherry blossom tea) is served to guests to represent new beginnings, just as the flower does in spring.

100g cherry blossom flowers
120g fine cooking salt
9 tablespoons plum or apple cider vinegar

1. Gently pick through your flowers, discarding any bugs, leaves or stalks. It's easiest to do this on your kitchen work surface and spread them out so you can see them all clearly.

2. Mix the flowers with the salt in a bowl and put a weight on them to release the water (ie. a plate with an unopened can or similar). Leave overnight. You will find that a blueish liquid will come out if you are using ornamental pink *Prunus serrulata*.

3. The following day you will need to gently wash the flowers. Fill up the bowl they are in with cold water and gently squeeze out the excess water, then place the flowers in another bowl. If they are in clumps then gently separate them, trying not to pull whole flowers apart. Sprinkle with the vinegar and again put a weight on the flowers and leave for three days, covering the bowl with a tea-towel.

4. After three days, place the flowers on kitchen paper and leave to dry for two days at room temperature. Keep the flowers in a sealed airtight sterilised jar.

CHERRY BLOSSOM SYRUP
Makes 1 x 750ml jar

I experimented with heating my sugar syrup to different temperatures to try to extract the best possible natural marzipan flavour from the cherry blossom flowers. I find anything between 50°C and 70°C (122–158°F) is a perfect heat for this. A sugar syrup made with equal parts water and sugar is sufficiently sweet to preserve, rather than ferment, the flowers.

80g cherry blossom flowers
600g caster sugar
600ml water

1. Gently pick through your flowers, discarding any bugs, stalks or leaves. Put the flowers in a 750ml jar that has been sterilised but is no longer hot.

2. Put the sugar and water in a saucepan and bring to the boil. Continue to boil until it reaches 100°C/212°F. Once it has reached this temperature, boil for a further 5 minutes, then remove from the heat and leave to rest and cool down to 70°C/158°F before pouring over the flowers. Pouring boiling syrup over the flowers will scorch the petals.

3. Seal immediately and leave to infuse for four weeks. Store in a cool dark place.

TIPS
To prepare cherry blossom tea, infuse the Salted Cherry Blossom in a teapot for 5 minutes. You may want to infuse for a shorter time depending on your desired taste.

Use the Cherry Blossom Syrup to flavour jams or pour over a flourless cake made with ground almonds.

GARIGUETTE STRAWBERRY & WHITE BALSAMIC JAM

Makes 6 x 220g jars

Originally from the south of France, the Gariguette strawberry is an early-season variety that is prized for its strong perfume. The berries are scarlet in colour and elongated in shape. During the month of May you will find them everywhere in Provence. Gariguette strawberries are becoming more common now as they can be easily grown, and are worth looking out for. I am going to be honest and say I have had some problems with strawberry jam as the fruit contain so little pectin, and I've spent years trying to create a recipe that would work without using additional pectin. Adding acid to the cooking process of jam (such as lemon or vinegar) binds with the sugar and natural fruit acid to form the gelling agent. This recipe is also a nod to my mum, who would serve her fresh unripe strawberries with balsamic vinegar and icing sugar back in the early nineties. Use white balsamic vinegar to retain the colour of the strawberries.

1.2kg Gariguette strawberries
800g caster sugar
100ml white balsamic vinegar
pinch of pink sea salt

1. Hull the strawberries and cut them in half. I like to keep them in halves so that you still have largish pieces when the jam is cooked.

2. Put the strawberries in a preserving pan and set over a low heat so that they start cooking and release some juice.

3. Slowly add the sugar, vinegar and salt and bring to the boil. Cook for 10 minutes or until the jam reaches setting point, 105°C/220°F on a sugar thermometer.

4. Remove from the heat and leave to rest for 5 minutes, stirring every few minutes so that the natural pectin is distributed evenly. Pour into warm sterilised jars and seal immediately. Store in a cool dark place.

TIPS
This jam is delicious served with goats' milk yogurt for breakfast or try making a set cream with goat's milk and cream.

If you can't get Gariguettes, then hold out until local strawberries are in season – patience is a virtue.

GORSE SYRUP

Makes 1 x 750ml jar

I first encountered gorse bushes while staying in Saddell Bay on the east coast of Kintyre, Scotland one spring. Walking along the beach I became aware of a strong coconut scent that instantly reminded me of my childhood in Australia during summertime. The scent from those bright yellow gorse flowers was so delicious they had to be edible – and indeed they are. I decided to pick a handful of flowers and test them out in a sugar syrup to see if I could extract that coconut flavour and it worked beautifully. You can also use the flowers raw, or to make a tea. Gorse bushes are really common in the British Isles, especially in coastal or windswept areas. Just be careful of your fingers when you pick the buds because the thorns are vicious.

80g gorse flowers
600g caster sugar
600ml water

1. Gently pick through your flowers, discarding any bugs or leaves. Put the flowers in a 750ml jar that has been sterilised but is no longer hot.

2. Put the sugar and water in a saucepan and bring to the boil. Boil until the temperature reaches 100°C/212°F on a sugar thermometer.

3. Continue to boil for a further 5 minutes, then remove from the heat and leave to rest and cool to 70°C/122F° before pouring over the flowers.

4. Seal immediately and leave for four weeks at room temperature. Once open, refrigerate and it will last for six months.

GORSE FLOWER WINE

Makes approx 6 x 750ml bottles

Making gorse wine takes time but the process is very satisfying and once you get around to drinking the wine a year later it tastes even more special. I like to make this quite sweet so you can serve it as you would a dessert wine. You need a lot of flowers so wear gloves to avoid painful jabs from the thorns and involve a few friends to make the process much quicker. Serve chilled.

2.5 litres gorse flowers
5 litres water
2kg caster sugar, plus 1 teaspoon
zest of 3 unwaxed oranges and 3 unwaxed lemons
5g white wine yeast

YOU WILL NEED:
Sterilised demijohn with an airlock, sterilised 10-litre plastic bucket (to sterilise, pour plenty of boiling water from the kettle into the bucket and roll it around to clean it thoroughly)

1. Gently pick through your flowers, discarding any bugs or leaves.

2. Put the water and sugar, reserving 1 teaspoon sugar, in a saucepan and bring to the boil, reduce the heat and simmer for 10 minutes, then remove from the heat.

3. Put the flowers and zest in the bucket. Pour over the hot water and sugar mixture. Allow to cool to blood temperature. Dissolve the yeast in warm water (37°C/98°F) with the remaining sugar.

4. Once the sugar/gorse mixture has cooled sufficiently, add the yeast mixture and stir well. Cover with a tea-towel and leave for four days, then strain off the citrus and gorse flowers and pour into a demijohn with an airlock. You will need to leave to ferment for around three months or until the yeast has completely evaporated through the airlock. The sign that it has done its job is when the liquid looks clear. Once clear, decant into sterilised wine bottles and leave for six months in a cool dark place, such as a cupboard or cellar.

'SMELLS LIKE COCONUT.'

TIPS

Serve Gorse Flower Wine at the end of a meal, or as part of a dessert: a scoop of vanilla ice cream with biscotti crumbled over the top and a little side glass of the wine to pour over the ice cream. Serve chilled.

It's really important to ensure the bucket is clean before you add the flowers and citrus zest otherwise unwanted bacteria might spoil your wine.

GREEN GOOSEBERRY & BAY LEAF JAM

Makes 6 x 220g jars

Gooseberry season starts with the firm, tart, green cooking variety, which I love to use for making a jam as the sharpness of the fruit counteracts the sugars, producing a not-so-sweet jam. Try to be aware of the sweetness of fruit when making jam and adjust your sugar levels accordingly: taste the fruit beforehand. Traditionally, the sign of elderflowers coming into bloom coincides with the appearance of green gooseberries and they do work beautifully together, but I think the warmth of bay leaves pairs equally well.

1.25kg green gooseberries
5 fresh bay leaves, torn
100ml water
800g caster sugar
juice of 1 lemon

1. Wash the gooseberries gently in cold water and top and tail them with a pair of scissors.

2. Put the fruit, whole, in a preserving pan and add the bay leaves and water. Set over a medium heat and cook the berries until they start to break down and the bay leaves start to release some of their flavours.

3. Add the sugar and lemon juice and boil until setting point is reached, 105°C/220°F on a sugar thermometer. Gooseberries are high in pectin so this jam should produce a thick-set jam. Once cooked, remove from the heat and pour straightaway into warm sterilised jars and seal immediately. Store in a cool dark place.

NOTES
Later-season gooseberries, more commonly known as dessert gooseberries, are often red, yellow or golden and are much sweeter than the early green ones.

The Egton Bridge Old Gooseberry Society in North Yorkshire holds a show each year on the first Tuesday in August where gooseberries compete for a place in the world records. Currently the largest on record weighs an impressive 62g.

PICKLED EARLY ROSE PETALS
Makes 1 x 500ml jar

In early spring, I'm on the hunt for colourful ingredients, ones that are edible and add some brightness to my meals. Rose petals tick that box. Look out for unsprayed early spring roses and don't use anything shop-brought as they tend to be farmed and have some nasties on them.

2 cups unsprayed rose petals
400ml apple cider vinegar
100g caster sugar
1 teaspoon sea salt
1 unwaxed lemon

1. Gently pull the petals from the flower heads and discard any insects or leaves. Place the petals in a cool sterilised jar; I like to use large Kilner-style jars for this but any that you have recycled will do.

2. Use a peeler to peel strips of lemon rind and place in the saucepan with the vinegar, sugar and salt and bring to the boil. Cook for 3 minutes or until the sugar has dissolved. Remove from the heat and leave to cool completely. (Pouring hot or warm liquid over the petals will discolour them and make them wilt.)

3. Once the liquid is cool, pour over the petals and seal immediately. Leave for five days before using. Once open, keep in the fridge for up to two weeks.

TIP
Once you have finished the petals, the liquid can be used for dressings or as a substitute for your everyday vinegar.

WILD GARLIC (RAMSON) PESTO

Makes 1 x 300g jar

I don't tend to make many savoury preserves as I use more flowers, herbs and fruit in the kitchen but wild garlic, or ramsons or ramps (as it is known in America), is one of those plants I pick every year and use in abundance. Every spring these alliums pop up, mostly growing in woodlands in masses as they like to self-seed. The distinctive garlic smell is a clear indication you've found them and tearing a leaf to release the scent is the best way to check this. Try and only pick a few leaves from each plant so that you don't over-pick.

80g wild garlic leaves
60g whole walnuts, roughly chopped
50g grated Parmesan
100ml extra virgin olive oil, plus extra
  for sealing the jars
sea salt and black pepper

1. Gently wash the wild garlic leaves and then leave to drain. Remove the excess water using a salad spinner or shake the leaves outside.

2. You can either make this using a pestle and mortar or an electric blender, pulsing it carefully so that you don't end up with a super smooth purée. If I am making a small batch then I use the pestle and mortar as that gives me more control over the texture, otherwise I use a blender, preparing all the ingredients before putting them in the blender so that the motor has less work to do. Slice the leaves and put them in a blender with the walnuts, Parmesan, half of the olive oil and some salt and pepper. Pulse until the mixture starts to break down then add the remainder of the oil.

3. Scoop the pesto into cool sterilised jars and top with extra olive oil to create a seal and stop the air spoiling the pesto. It will keep for up to two months in the fridge as long as it's always covered with oil.

PINK ELDERFLOWER & SAGE VINEGAR

(BLACK LACE ELDERBERRY)

Makes 1 x 1.5-litre jar

If you ask around, you might be lucky enough to find someone who has an elderflower tree producing pink blooms rather than the more common creamy white ones. Both will work equally well in this recipe, although the pink ones will produce a prettier coloured vinegar. Always try to pick elderflowers well away from roads and urban centres to avoid the pollution.

3 cups pink elderflower heads
5 sage leaves
peel of 1 unwaxed lemon
1.5 litres raw unfiltered apple cider vinegar`

1. Trim the main stalks off the elderflowers but leave the heads whole. Pick out any bugs from the flowers but do not wash or shake the heads as you will lose the flavoursome pollen.

2. Put the flowers in a large sterilised jar with the sage leaves, lemon peel and vinegar. Seal and leave to infuse for one month and then strain.

TIP
Use as you would any other vinegar but don't cook with it or you will lose its vibrant pink colour and delicate flavour.

ELDERFLOWER &
LOVAGE BUBBLES

Makes 4 x 1 litre bottles

I've made many batches of elderflower bubbles and have learned through experience that you need to be a little more attentive than I was in the past. For instance, if you go on holiday, you need the help of friends who can release the pressure that the natural yeast creates, otherwise you risk returning to exploded bottles. I have suffered much anxiety over these bottles and the fear of them bursting! You need to use either sturdy glass bottles that have a good clasp or plastic bottles with screwtop lids.

Elderflowers are packed with natural yeasts, although sometimes the mix needs a kick-start. If it shows no signs of fermentation after three days, you may need to give it some help and add a champagne yeast.

6 elderflower heads
3.5 litres water, plus 500ml hot water
   for dissolving the sugar
2 tablespoons raw unfiltered apple cider vinegar
rind and juice of 2 unwaxed lemons
20g lovage leaves, torn into pieces
750g caster sugar

YOU WILL NEED:
Sterilised 10-litre plastic bucket, (to sterilise, pour plenty of boiling water from the kettle into the bucket and roll it around to clean it thoroughly), 4 x sterilised 1-litre bottles

1. Ensure all your equipment is as clean as possible, especially the large bucket you will use for your first fermentation, so give this a really good clean in hot soapy water before sterlising.

2. Pick out any bugs from the flowers but do not wash or shake the heads as you will lose the flavoursome pollen. Put the flowers in the sterilised bucket with the water, vinegar, lemon rind and juice and the lovage leaves.

3. Put the sugar in a large bowl with the remaining 500ml hot water. Stir to dissolve and allow to cool, then add to the bucket.

4. Leave to infuse for four days. Strain the liquid and pour into sterilised bottles and cap immediately. It should take about seven to ten days to become fizzy but start checking after five days by slowly releasing the cap and then check every day. It may take longer than ten days for the yeasts to develop, depending on the temperature.

GIANT HIBISCUS FLOWER
ICE CUBES

Makes 1–2 ice-cube trays, depending on size

Hibiscus flowers offer a really vibrant natural red food dye that can be used for colouring many sweets and desserts. I use dried hibiscus flowers in my raspberry jam to help retain the colour and also add some acidity to overly sweet berries cooked into sugar. Here, I made a simple cordial with them and then froze it into giant ice cube trays to add some fun to drinks. You could also try freezing some of the flowers in the cubes.

750ml water
200g caster sugar
3 tablespoons dried hibiscus flowers

1. Put the water and sugar in a saucepan, bring to the boil, then reduce the heat to a simmer. Tear up the hibiscus flowers and add them to the sugar syrup.

2. Simmer the cordial over a low heat for 5 minutes, then remove from the heat.

3. Leave to completely cool and then strain, pouring into your favourite ice-cube trays. Freeze overnight.

LOQUAT & SWEET CICELY JAM
LOQUATS, NESPOLE, GOLDEN NUGGET, MALTA ERIĞI (MALTESE PLUM)

Makes 8 x 220g jars

Most of my food pairing comes down to me going out into my garden and seeing what is growing at the time of my fruit purchase. This year, spring was four weeks earlier than the previous year, which meant my garden was flourishing and my sweet cicely had just flowered. I decided not to use the flowers in this jam recipe, just the green parts, as I wanted to dry the flowers into a pollen for scattering into jam I make later in the year. Loquats are a stone fruit originally from China and the succulent flesh is sweet and tangy. Make sure you use young ripe loquats here; I have tried to make this later in the season and it doesn't work as well as the loquats don't break down as easily when you cook them.

1.8kg loquats
250ml water
2 handfuls of sweet cicely leaves
1kg caster sugar
juice of 1 lemon

1. To clean your loquats place them in water, cut them in half and pop out the two silky stones. If there are any brown fibrous bits at the ends cut these off too.

2. After cleaning and stoning the loquats you should have 1.5kg of fruit left. Place them in a preserving pan and add the water and set over a medium heat.

3. Cover the pan with a lid and gently simmer until the fruit softens, then add the sweet cicely, sugar and lemon juice and bring to the boil.

4. Bring the jam to the boil and cook until setting point, 105°C/220°F on a sugar thermometer. Remove the pan from the heat and leave to rest for 5 minutes stirring to distribute any bubbles – these will slowly disappear.

5. Pour into warm sterilised jars and seal immediately. Store in a cool dark place.

CANDIED ANGELICA

Makes 1 x 1-litre jar

I have had numerous angelica plants growing in my garden over the years and it has been a bit of a learning curve. The first one I planted went straight to seed the following year and then disappeared. I remember chatting to a friend about it and she said that when they go to seed that means they have finished, and she was right. If you manage to cut the flowers before it goes to seed then you should get another year out of the plant. The best time of year to harvest the smaller tender stalks is in spring, just before they start growing again and become tough. The leafy parts can be torn up and popped into some sugar to flavour them.

500g young angelica stalks, washed and cut into pieces about 10cm/4in long
½ teaspoon baking powder
550g caster sugar
550ml water
caster sugar, for coating (optional)

1. Put the angelica stalks in a saucepan and add enough water to cover, along with the baking powder. Bring to the boil, then reduce the heat to a gentle simmer and cook until the stalks are tender, about 8–10 minutes.

2. Drain the stalks and plunge into a bowl of iced water to stop the cooking process. Once cool, strain the stalks and peel with a small paring knife to remove any fibrous skin (any very young stalks won't have long fibre strands).

3. Put the sugar and water in a heavy-based saucepan, bring to the boil and add the prepared angelica. Simmer for 20 minutes or until tender and the syrup is reduced and thick. Remove from the heat, leave to rest for 5 minutes then strain off the syrup.

4. If you wish to dry and roll in sugar for crystallised pieces, then strain the angelica from the syrup and roll each piece in caster sugar, if using, and place on a flat tray lined with parchment paper to dry out overnight in an ambient kitchen. Reserve the leftover syrup to flavour summer drinks or boil into your jams. Store the dried angelica pieces in an airtight jar. If you prefer not to roll in sugar, then store in the syrup and use as you need.

TIPS
Cassata cake, above, born in Palermo in Sicily, is traditionally decorated with candied fruit. You could decorate your cakes with candied angelica.

I like to dice up the candied angelica and cook it with my jams so that I get little chewy jewels that taste like juniper berries (page 58).

RHUBARB, PISTACHIO & ORANGE BLOSSOM JAM

Makes 10 x 300ml jars

I love outdoor-grown rhubarb as it really is the gift that keeps on giving. You can plant a crown in your garden and it will come back year after year, providing you with endless supplies of earthy tasting stalks. I adore the sharpness of this vegetable, and cooked with sugar it's a marriage made for my palate – the sweetness bringing out the earthiness without being overly sour or sweet.

1.2kg outdoor-grown rhubarb, washed and chopped into 5cm/2in pieces
200ml water
800g caster sugar
50g pistachios (shelled weight)
juice of 1 lemon
2 tablespoons orange blossom water

1. Put the rhubarb in a heavy-based saucepan with the water and set over a medium heat.

2. Once the rhubarb has started to break down, gradually add the sugar, pistachios and lemon juice, stirring to combine.

3. Bring the jam to the boil and cook until the jam reaches setting point, 105°C/220°F on a sugar thermometer.

4. Remove from the heat, add the orange blossom water and leave to rest for 5 minutes, stirring to distribute any bubbles – these will slowly disappear. Pour into warm sterilised jars and seal immediately. Store in a cold dark place.

TIPS
For breakfast rhubarb, slow-roast rhubarb stalks in a low oven (120°C/250°F/gas mark ½) for approx. 30 minutes with some sugar, sweet cicely and any warm spices you may have in your cupboard. Keeping the oven low will help ensure the stalks are nice and firm – just keep double checking that they don't overcook.

PICKLED GREEN ALMONDS
Makes 1 x 1 litre jar

Green almonds are a sign that almond trees have started to develop their fruit for the season. These furry green oval-shaped nuts have not yet developed into hard almonds and are perfect for slicing up raw or pickling. Look out for crunchy young tender almonds in early to mid-spring – those that have a soft shell and a jelly-like centre when you slice them open are best as once they start to ripen and the shell becomes harder they will be much harder to pickle.

500g young green almonds
4 bay leaves
550ml water
450ml raw unfiltered apple cider vinegar
2 tablespoons salt
50g caster sugar

1. Wipe the almonds with a clean cloth. Pierce them with a skewer down one side three or four times (this will help them absorb the pickling liquid) and put in a sterilised jar with the bay leaves.

2. Put the water, vinegar, salt and sugar in a heavy-based saucepan and bring to the boil. Reduce the heat and simmer for 5 minutes. Remove from the heat and leave to cool for 5 minutes.

3. Pour the pickling liquid over the almonds and seal immediately. Leave for one month in a cool dark place, before using. Refrigerate once opened.

TIPS
You can pop out the soft almond-like kernel and cook these through your jams or into stewed fruit.

Braise whole green almonds with olive oil, stock, fennel tops, lemon zest, garlic and salt and serve as an appetiser. Again, you need very young almonds for this.

APRICOT & KERNEL JAM
Makes 7 x 220g jars

Removing kernels from their stones takes patience and arm strength. You will need to be careful how you do this as you need to break the stone not the tips of your fingers. It works best if you individually wrap the stones in a tea-towel and hit them with a hammer so that fragments of stone don't go flying around your kitchen or into your jam prep. Try to work out a firm smash that isn't super hard so you don't squash the almond-like kernel inside, which is much softer than the stone.

1.5kg apricots
200ml water
900g caster sugar
juice of 1 lemon

1. Remove any stalks and halve the apricots so that you can pop out the stones. Put the apricot halves in a preserving pan with the water.

2. To extract the kernels, wrap each stone individually in a tea-towel and give it a sharp bang with a hammer, making sure your spare hand is away from the stone – you should be able to do this with one hard hit!

3. Once you have popped out all the kernels, check carefully and discard any shell pieces. I like to cut the kernels up a little so that they will release more flavour when cooking in the jam but you can leave them whole if you prefer.

4. Add the kernels to the pan with the apricots and water and slowly bring to a gentle simmer. Cook until the apricots start to break down. Add the sugar and lemon juice, bring to the boil and cook until the jam reaches setting point, 105°C/220°F on a sugar thermometer. Remove from the heat and leave to rest for 5 minutes before pouring into warm sterilised jars, and sealing immediately. Store in a cool dark place.

> TIPS
> Pop your kernels into some vodka to make an intense almond essence.
>
> You can also infuse the kernels into custards, ice creams and sorbets. Try making a custard base and cook the kernels through it. Leave for 24 hours, then strain. You will notice a subtle marzipan (noyaux) like flavour.

EARLY RASPBERRY & ANISE HYSSOP JAM
Makes 7 x 220g jars

Continuing in my bid to encourage you to grow more herbs and plants in your space, anise hyssop is hard to find and it will be much easier trying to grow this herb rather than sourcing it. Anise hyssop looks similar to mint and has purple flowers and sometimes purple leaves. The flavour is a cross between mint and anise – more similar to fennel seeds. You can also try drying anise hyssop if you have a large harvest. This results in a slightly different flavour, which I think is better suited to savoury dishes.

1kg raspberries
600g caster sugar
1 cup anise hyssop leaves (you can also use the flowers
   if you have them), torn
juice of 1 lemon

1. Combine the raspberries, sugar and anise hyssop in a bowl, mix thoroughly and cover with a tea-towel. Leave to macerate overnight – this helps to draw out the flavour of the anise hyssop.

2. The following day, put all the macerated ingredients in a heavy-based pan, add the lemon juice and set over a medium heat, stirring so that it doesn't catch on the base.

3. Bring to the boil and cook until the jam reaches setting point, 105°C/220°F on a sugar thermometer. You don't need to rest this jam so you can pour straight away into warm sterilised jars and seal immediately. Store in a cool dark place.

TIP
Try substituting anise hyssop with mint or lemon balm. Early raspberry varieties might include Glen Clova, Glen Moy and Malling Promise.

CHERRY & BLACK PEPPER JAM

Makes 7 x 220g jars

I bought a manual cherry stoner in the south of France a few years ago and it has been one of the best pieces of equipment I've purchased. It has helped provide me with many pots of cherry jam that would otherwise have taken triple the time to make. If you can find one of these, or even a handheld one, I would highly recommend it. You will probably still find a few stray stones in your jam but once it starts boiling these will come to the surface and you can scoop them out easily. Another thought is to gather a few friends together and feed them wine in exchange for cherry stoning. This tends to work well when the weather is nice.

2kg cherries
5g black peppercorns
1.1kg caster sugar
200g Green Apple Stock Jelly (see page 160)
juice of 1 lemon

1. Wash the cherries in cold water and pick off all the stems. Strain them in a sieve, making sure all excess water is drained.

2. Use a cherry stoner to remove the stones. Put the cherries in a heavy-based saucepan, set over a low heat and start cooking them gently until they start releasing some liquid and begin to break down.

3. Gently grind the black peppercorns using a pestle and mortar until you have a coarse powder. Add this to the pan.

4. Once the cherries appear to have started stewing, slowly start adding the sugar, stirring to dissolve, then add the jelly and lemon juice. Bring to the boil and cook the jam until setting point is reached, 105°C/220°F on a sugar thermometer.

5. Remove from the heat and leave to rest for 3 minutes, stirring to distribute the cherries, and then pour into warm sterilised jars and seal immediately. Store in a cool dark place.

TIPS
Always sample cherries before you buy them as flavourless cherries make a flavourless jam that ends up only tasting of sugar.

Look out for plump juicy cherries that will drop some liquid when cooked.

PEACH & FIG LEAF JAM
Makes 7 x 220g jars

Ensure you use really ripe peaches for this – or indeed any peach jam recipe. If the fruit is too hard it won't cook down in the sugar and you will end up with hard pieces of fruit, not a luscious glossy jam. Peaches in late spring do tend to be firmer as they won't have seen much sun. Even if you buy firmer peaches, be sure to leave them out to ripen on a sunny window or place them in a paper bag, which speeds up the process.

1.5kg ripe peaches, halved and stoned
5 early fig leaves, torn into pieces
900g caster sugar
juice of 1 lemon

1. Cut each peach half into quarters and place in a preserving pan with the fig leaves. If the peaches are not super soft, add a splash of water to help them break down. It might help to place a lid on the pan to speed up the cooking process. It's really important that the peaches are cooked through before you add the sugar, so test them by piercing with a knife to check for softness.

2. Once the peaches are soft, add the sugar and lemon juice and cook until the jam reaches setting point, 105°C/220°F on a sugar thermometer. Remove from the heat and leave to rest for 5 minutes before pouring into warm sterilised jars and seal immediately. Store in a cool dark place.

TIP
If you're looking for a more caramelised flavour, try roasting the peaches in the oven at 120°C/250°F/gas mark ½ for an hour, alongside a quarter of the sugar. This will help the fruit to soften and the sugars turn brown. Then cook as above, adding the sugar once the fruit has broken down.

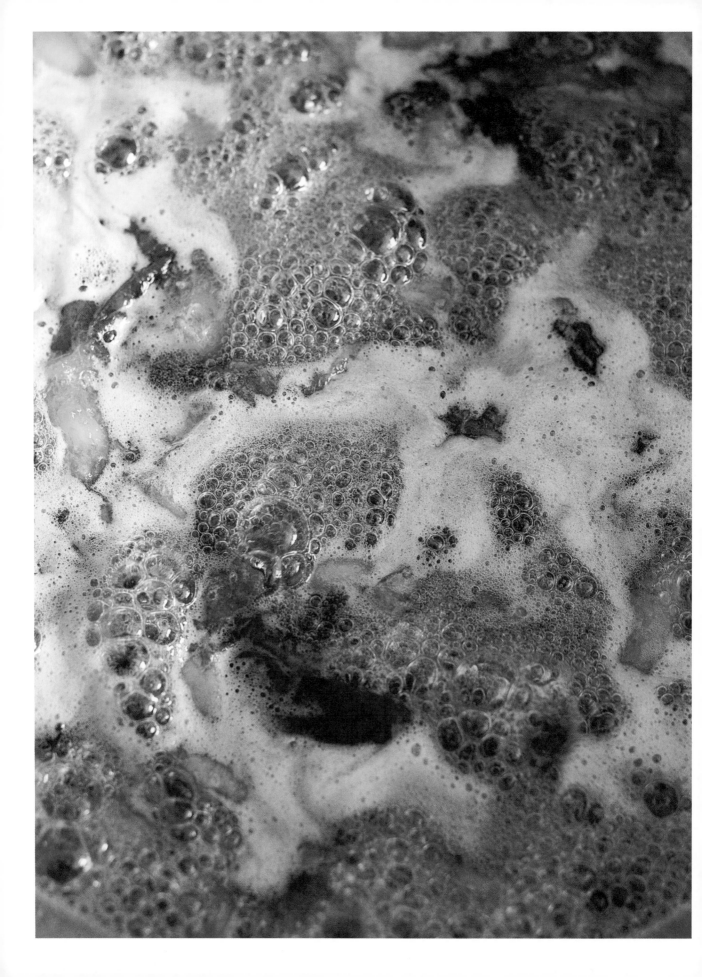

SWEET

TART

VIVID

BRIGHT

STICKY

H

GOING

PICKING

Until the 1960s, many of London's East End's working class families would travel to Kent each summer to work in the many orchards and hop farms that once dominated the rural landscape. They would spend the whole season picking, packing and processing the fruit and hops before returning to London with their working wages. The advance of agricultural mechanisation has meant that manual labour is no longer the most popular choice for commercial growers on a larger scale, and the demise of many small farms has meant less helping hands are required, although there are still many farms that need people to pick in the summer months.

Many fruit growers still exist throughout England and families now make day trips out to pick-your-own (PYO) farms. I like to spend time during my jamming season (spring, summer and autumn) seeking out PYO farms to find more unusual fruit: loganberries, tayberries, gooseberries, boysenberries, whitecurrants, many plum varieties, cobnuts and, if I'm lucky, the occasional mulberry. It's possible to track down some of these hard-to-find treasures at a local farmers' market or, if you have some green space, it may be worth planting some of these special fruit. Sadly, few commercial enterprises are interested in growing the more unusual varieties. Finding bulk fruit for jam-making can also be a little tricky. PYO farms will almost certainly guarantee you a nice harvest of fruit if not better quality fruit and a sun tan. Bring your hat.

These days, 'going picking' can mean more than harvesting fruit in Kent. Since opening my small shop in East London, I have worked with a company called Company Drinks, an arts project and community drinks enterprise linking East London's tradition of going picking with a full drinks-production cycle; from picking to bottling, branding to trading and reinvesting. The drinks are made with fruit, flowers and herbs picked by locals and the range includes sodas, cordials, birch sap, ciders and a green hop tonic. Founded by my local neighbour, Kathrin Böhm, Company Drinks was set up as an example of how to combine local heritage (going picking and the area's agricultural and industrial past) with local resources (surplus fruit, growing spaces, local skills and a local economy).

'I like to spend time during my jamming season
(spring, summer and autumn) seeking out PYO
farms to find more unusual fruit.'

So far, more than 36,000 people from across London have got involved in events run by Company Drinks. Over 2,400 Barking and Dagenham residents have taken part in picking trips and walks, more than 1,000 young people have learned about making and mixing drinks, and they have held more than 46 monthly 'Hopping Afternoons' based on the history and celebrations of hop picking. Company Drinks runs community-based workshops throughout the picking year, including blackcurrant gleaning (the word for gathering the remaining crop after the main harvest), which I joined.

Another workshop run by Company Drinks is one that I am particularly fascinated by – the invasive Japanese knotweed, which, it turns out, is edible. When picked safely in areas where it hasn't been chemically sprayed, this highly invasive weed makes a delicious-tasting soda or can be cooked the same way as you would rhubarb, both offering a similar earthy taste. Japanese knotweed is so destructive that there is no way of ever over-harvesting it. In fact, we're doing this plant and our landscapes a massive favour by trying to utilise it in our diet. Identifying Japanese knotweed is pretty easy: its stalks look like pinkish-green bamboo and it has lime green large teardrop-shaped leaves. Try using the young tender stalks before they get too big and woody, otherwise you will find it hard trying to cook it down. Like most stems, you need to pick them early on in the season.

NOTE
Japanese knotweed shouldn't be picked without permission from your local council so double check with them before picking and/or contact Company Drinks and tag along to one of their workshops so that you can learn about this amazing weed and how to use it safely.

LOGANBERRY & CANDIED ANGELICA JAM

Makes 5 x 220g jars

Every mid-summer for the past four years a lovely man called Mark has ridden his bike from South London all the way to my small shop in Clapton, East London, to drop off kilos of fresh juicy loganberries. Mark knows me from my days when I had a stall at my local Chatsworth Road market and appreciates how much I love these berries. Out of the love of his heart he makes this trek every year to his local farmers' market stall and visits a wonderful lady named Leila who is a grower of loganberries – they seem to have agreement where she saves them all for him, perhaps knowing this story? She doesn't seem to mind though. In return I make him a supply of jam that will last all year but I think he may give most of it away as gifts. We don't even swap phone numbers. These sweet berries make a wonderful jam with the herby taste of angelica – hopefully you'll have enough left from candying it in the spring.

1kg loganberries
50g Candied Angelica (see page 36), drained from its syrup and
   sliced into 5mm/¼in pieces
700g caster sugar
juice of 1 lemon

1. Put the loganberries and angelica in a heavy-based saucepan and set over a low heat. Cook for 5 minutes to release the fruit juices along with the flavour from the angelica.

2. Slowly add the sugar and lemon juice, bring to the boil and cook for 10 minutes or until the jam reaches setting point, 105°C/220°F on a sugar thermometer. Pour into warm sterilised jars and seal immediately. Store in a cool dark place.

NOTE
Loganberries are a blackberry x raspberry hybrid with the shape of a blackberry but the colour of a raspberry.

STRAWBERRY & WILD FENNEL POLLEN JAM
Makes 6 x 220g jars

Every summer I pick an abundance of the wild fennel growing on the sides of the trusty railway line near my home in London. It's native to the Mediterranean but seems to be naturalised around the world. It spreads along railway lines and in dry regions along roadsides and beaches. Considering the price of dried fennel pollen, I highly recommend picking wild fennel (don't worry about over-picking this invasive plant as it self-seeds prolifically). You can hang it upside down to dry out at home, then trim off the fragrant dried flower heads full of pollen and keep them in an airtight container – they will last until the following year's harvest. I like to use the flower heads, both fresh and dried, in my jams to create an anise/liquorice taste.

1.2kg strawberries
1 cup fresh wild fennel flower heads
** (or 1 teaspoon dried wild fennel pollen)**
800g caster sugar
juice of 1 lemon

1. Hull the strawberries and cut them in half. Depending on size, I like to keep them in halves so that you still have largish pieces when the jam is cooked.

2. Put the strawberries in a heavy-based saucepan and set over a low heat so that they start to cook and release some juice.

3. Use a pair of scissors to snip off the tops of the fennel flowers and add them to the pan – it's easiest to do this over the pan.

4. Slowly add the sugar and lemon juice and bring to the boil. Cook for 10 minutes or until the jam reaches setting point, 105°C/220°F on a sugar thermometer. Remove from the heat and leave to rest for 5 minutes, stirring every few minutes so that the natural pectin is distributed evenly. Pour into warm sterilised jars and seal immediately. Store in a cool dark place.

TIP
Once the fennel stalks have been dried out carefully, shake over a big bowl so as to catch all the pollen. This is the more potent part of the plant so treat it like gold dust.

TAYBERRY & CHERRY BLOSSOM JAM
Makes 5 x 220g jars

Tayberries are another summer fruit that I like to pick for my summer jams. At a quick glance they could be mistaken for loganberries as they are a similar cross between a blackberry and raspberry – in fact the fruit was bred to be an improvement on the loganberry at a Scottish horticultural institute in Dundee and the name comes from the river Tay, which is where the institute is located. Tayberries are more aromatic and sweeter than loganberries. The big difference between these two berries for me is the flavour and sweetness levels, so it's best to try them on the day of picking to see how they taste and adjust your sugar levels accordingly. Try experimenting with some of your spring sugar syrups here, but only ever use the one syrup otherwise the flavour will be lost if you start combining.

1kg tayberries
500g caster sugar
150ml Cherry Blossom Syrup (see page 20)
juice of 1 lemon

1. Put the tayberries in a heavy-based saucepan and set over a low heat. Cook for 5 minutes to release the juices.

2. Slowly add the sugar, syrup and lemon juice, bring to the boil and cook for 10 minutes or until the jam reaches setting point, 105°C/220°F on a sugar thermometer. Pour into warm sterilised jars and seal immediately. Store in a cool dark place.

TIPS
Substitute the cherry blossom syrup for salted cherry blossom flowers (see page 20). Just add an extra 150g of sugar in place of the sweet syrup.

Try baking this jam into some biscuits like these thumbprint ones in the photograph opposite.

BOYSENBERRY & NASTURTIUM JAM
Makes 5 x 220g jars

Boysenberries take me back to my childhood growing up in Melbourne, Australia. I had never come across them in the UK until I was driving home from a weekend in Sussex and passed a PYO farm sign on a motorway and did a swift U-turn to go and see what they had available. I don't think it's possible for me to drive past a PYO farm and not stop – the thought of missing out on something special is unbearable! I'm so happy I stopped that day as I found someone finally growing my treasured and nostalgia-filled boysenberries. This delicious berry is a cross between a blackberry, a raspberry, an American dewberry and a loganberry. They lean more towards a blackberry and are much plumper and sweeter. The sweet and tart flavour makes them ideal for jam-making.

1kg boysenberries
1 cup small nasturtium leaves
600g caster sugar
juice of 1 lemon

1. Put the boysenberries and nasturtium leaves in a heavy-based saucepan and set over a low heat. Cook for 5 minutes to release the juices and the peppery flavour from the nasturtium leaves.

2. Slowly add the sugar and lemon juice, bring to the boil and cook for 10 minutes or until the jam reaches setting point, 105°C/220°F on a sugar thermometer. Pour into warm sterilised jars and seal immediately. Store in a cool dark place.

TIP
Seeking out boysenberries might be a trial but that's the fun, isn't it? Your best bet is checking in with your local PYO farms. Boysenberries aren't generally grown for retail as they don't have a long shelf life. If you have the space, they're very easy to grow and are less invasive than raspberries and blackberries. As a bonus, the stems are thornless.

MORELLO CHERRY & PISTACHIO JAM

Makes 7 x 220g jars

Morello cherries, known in French as *griottes*, are a traditional cooking cherry with a sour taste, perfect for making jam and for using in baking and cooking. These may be hard to find in shops so the best solution may be to visit a PYO farm or plant your own tree. Any cherry variety will work but taste them first for flavour. If they are too sweet your jam will end up being overwhelmingly sugary. You want sour-tasting cherries that have a more full-bodied flavour. Cherries contain very little pectin so I like to make this jam in really small batches. This allows you to cook quickly and reach the required setting point without the jam over-boiling and becoming too sweet.

1.6kg morello cherries
700g caster sugar
250g green apple stock jelly (see page 160)
150g green pistachio slivers
juice of 1 lemon

1. Carefully stone the cherries and weigh the fruit – you should have about 1.5kg. Once you've finished, run your fingers through the fruit to check whether you can feel any stones. Don't worry if you miss a few as once the jam starts cooking any stones will come to the surface and you can scoop them out with a spoon.

2. Put the stoned cherries in a heavy-based saucepan, set over a medium heat, cover with a lid and cook for 5 minutes or until they become soft. Be careful not to let the juices evaporate as the point of cooking these is to release their juices.

3. Slowly add the sugar, jelly, pistachios and lemon juice, bring to the boil and cook rapidly for 10 minutes or until the jam reaches setting point, 105°C/220°F on a sugar thermometer. Pour into warm sterilised jars and seal immediately. Store in a cool dark place.

TIP
If, like me, you love cherries, you may want to invest in a cherry stoner. If you already have an olive stoner it will work really well for smaller batches of cherries but if you have an overload of fruit it might be worth investing in a small manual cherry stoner. I picked up mine in France at a wholesale food and drink supplier but you can buy them online.

WHITECURRANT & LEMON BALM JELLY

Makes 10 x 220g jars

Resembling translucent pearls of caviar and with names like White Grape and Versailles Blanche, it is a little heartbreaking to boil up these little jewels and watch them turn into a pulp, but the result is a ruby-pink clear jelly that is so pretty it seems acceptable. Like redcurrants, whitecurrants are very easy to grow and are almost identical, the only differences being the colour and the fact that they are sweeter in taste.

1.4kg whitecurrants
3.3 litres water
1 cup of lemon balm, leaves and stalks
1.4kg caster sugar

1. Put the whitecurrants and water in a heavy-based saucepan and bring to the boil. Reduce the heat to a simmer and cook for 20 minutes without mashing up the fruit too much as this will affect the clearness of the jelly.

2. Once the pulp is cooked, strain through a cheesecloth-lined colander set over a large bowl and leave overnight.

3. The following day, discard the pulp (put into your compost) and measure the strained liquid – you should end up with about 2.3–2.5 litres of clear liquid.

4. Pour the liquid into a preserving pan, add the lemon balm and bring to the boil. Slowly add the sugar and boil for about 25 minutes until setting point is reached. A good indication that it is ready is if you stir the boiling liquid with a wooden spoon and find that all the bubbles rise up and seem to overflow and the bubbles start to look more like foam.

5. Once setting point is reached, don't delay leaving the jelly in the pan as it will start to set immediately. Pour quickly into a large jug, leave for 2 minutes and then skim off the top. (The top is where the bubbles will rise and start setting, if you skim this off you wont have any bubbles in the jelly.) Pour into warm sterilised jars and seal immediately. Store in a cool dark place.

PÊCHE DE VIGNE & LEMON JAM

Makes 8 x 220g jars

Pêche de vigne translates as 'peach of the grapevine' and the name of this peach variety refers to an old tradition in the Lyon region of France where grape growers used to plant a peach tree at the ends of their rows of vines. These peaches are as exciting as opening a perfectly ripe pomegranate or cutting into the bloodiest blood orange – it's all about the surprise of finding that the flesh can be a deep red in contrast to the skin of the fruit. If you can't find pêches de vigne, then try and find white peaches, which are more readily available. You want perfectly ripe peaches so leave them out to ripen if they are too hard.

1.8kg Pêches de Vigne peaches (about 11 peaches), halved and stoned
1kg caster sugar
zest of 2 unwaxed lemons and juice of 1 lemon

1. Cut each peach half into quarters. Dice into 2cm/¾in cubes and put in a heavy-based saucepan. If the peaches are not super soft, add a little water to help them break down, about 250ml. It might help to cover the pan with a lid to speed up the cooking process; it's really important that the peaches are cooked through before you add the sugar.

2. Once the peaches are soft, slowly add the sugar, lemon zest and juice and cook for 10 minutes or until the jam reaches setting point, 105°C/220°F on a sugar thermometer. Remove from the heat and leave to rest for 5 minutes before pouring into warm sterilised jars and sealing immediately. Store in a cool dark place.

TIP
It's really important to use the ripest stone fruit when making jams so that they break down quickly and gel with the sugar. If you don't you will end up with hard pieces of fruit and a sugar syrup instead of a jam.

RASPBERRY & LIQUORICE JAM

Makes 5 x 220g jars

This is one of my classic jams that I made when I first started experimenting back in 2011. At the beginning I used pure liquorice pellets from Calabria in Italy that are incredibly strong but take some time to melt down in the jam. Then I switched to soft liquorice, which, when cut into small pieces, melts down. If you wish, cut it into bigger pieces so that they stay solid after cooking, which is a nice little surprise at the bottom of the jar.

1kg raspberries
60g soft liquorice, cut into 1cm/½in pieces
600g caster sugar
juice of 1 lemon

1. Put the raspberries and liquorice in a heavy-based saucepan and set over a low heat. Cook for 5 minutes to release the juices and partially melt the liquorice, stirring so that the liquorice doesn't stick to the bottom of the pan.

2. Slowly add the sugar and lemon juice and bring to the boil. Cook for 10 mintues or until the jam reaches setting point, 105°C/220°F on a sugar thermometer. Pour into warm sterilised jars and seal immediately. Store in a cool dark place.

TIP
You can use liquorice with any berries: try it with blackberries for a richer, bolder flavour at the end of summer when the blackberries are nice and plump.

BLACKCURRANT LEAF WINE
Makes 1 x 1 litre jar

The leaves from the blackcurrant bush are an extra bonus as their flavour is nearly as intense as the currants themselves. Using more than one part of a plant is an exciting departure from the norm but also an eco- and cost-friendly way of reducing the amount we waste. Blackcurrant leaves can add their flavour to many recipes including custards, ice-cream bases and sorbets. I like to include a few in my jam. Try infusing the leaves in a sugar syrup as I have done with cherry blossom and gorse flowers (see pages 20 and 24) .

This recipe infuses leftover red wine into a sweet liqueur that is both perfect for drinking with lots of ice or serving with fresh strawberries. Use leaves that haven't been sprayed with chemicals and pick them when the fruit is ripe.

30 blackcurrant leaves
750ml red wine (try using leftovers or buy a fruity
   variety, such as Sangiovese or Beaujolais)
85g demerara sugar
150ml cassis
rind of 1 unwaxed orange

1. Wash the leaves and strain off the excess water. Put the leaves in a 1-litre wide-rimmed sterilised jar.

2. Add the wine, sugar, cassis and orange peel and put the lid on the jar. Leave at room temperature for seven days, stirring every few days to help the sugar dissolve. After seven days, strain the wine and decant into a glass bottle with an airtight lid and use as you need. It will keep in the fridge for up to six months.

TIPS
Serve blackcurrant leaf wine chilled over ice with a slice of orange on a hot summer's day.

Pour the wine over fresh strawberries for a quick, light dessert with fresh basil.

YELLOW NECTARINE & FLOWERING THYME JAM
Makes 7 x 220g jars

Nectarines and peaches are very similar except that the skin of peaches is furry whereas nectarines have soft shiny skin. Some people like to peel their stone fruit but lots of the natural colour is in the skin – the blush alone can be enough to turn a jam from yellow to a pink shade. Nectarines will vary for the whole season, starting firmer and, as the sun gets hotter, plumper and juicier – these are the ones to look out for, really soft and ripe. The best way to test is to bite into one and see if the juices start flowing.

1.5kg ripe nectarines (about 10 nectarines),
   halved and stoned
¼ cup thyme flowers
900g caster sugar
pinch of sea salt
juice of 1 lemon

1. Slice each nectarine half into 4 slices and then dice into 2cm/¾in cubes. Place these into a heavy-based saucepan along with the thyme flowers and set over a medium heat. Cook for about 15 minutes or until soft to touch.

2. Slowly add the sugar, salt and lemon juice and cook for 10 minutes or until the jam reaches setting point, 105°C/220°F on a sugar thermometer.

3. Remove from the heat and leave to rest for 5 minutes before pouring into warm sterilised jars and sealing immediately. Store in a cool dark place.

JOSTABERRY JAM
Makes 7 x 220g jars

My first encounter with jostaberries came only recently when the lovely Jane Scotter at Fern Verrow, a farm on the English-Welsh border, contacted me to see if I would be interested in using some for jam-making. Jostaberries are a cross between a gooseberry and a blackcurrant, which makes them a little less intense than a blackcurrant. Eaten raw, the flavour is similar to gooseberry but, once cooked, it becomes more intensified and leans more towards blackcurrant. When I discover a new fruit I tend to leave it solo for my first few batches of jam in order to familiarise myself with the flavour. Only then might I pair it with a friend, but I have decided to keep the jostaberry solo because it is a cross-fruit and I like to think you will discover both flavours. Look out at farmers' markets or on PYO farms for jostaberries. Jostaberries are high in pectin so you will find this an easy jam to cook which doesn't need long on the heat.

1.5kg jostaberries
1kg caster sugar
juice of 1 lemon

1. Remove the stalks and the little tuft from the jostaberries. I find it easiest to fill up the sink with water, put the berries in the water to wash and prep at the same time, then drain in a colander or sieve.

2. Put the jostaberries in a heavy-based saucepan and cook over a low heat until they start to break down and release some of the juices. This should take about 5 minutes.

3. Slowly add the sugar and lemon juice, bring to the boil and cook for 10 minutes or until the jam reaches setting point, 105°C/220°F on a sugar thermometer. Pour into warm sterilised jars and seal immediately. Store in a cool dark place.

TIPS
Prepping jostaberries is as labour intensive as topping and tailing gooseberries, so ensure you have a bit of time on your hands when you decide to make this jam.

If you can't find jostaberries, then substitute half and half with red gooseberries and blackcurrants. Even though I don't like to mix any fruit together, I will allow it here!

TIP
Use sour pickled cherries as you would any pickle. Serve
with game meats or stir through some whipped cream and
broken-up meringue for an easy dessert – but remember
there are stones in the fruit.

SOUR PICKLED CHERRIES & FENNEL TOPS

Makes 1 x 1 litre jar

You don't need to use any specific cherry variety for this recipe but look out for larger cherries as they will be infusing in a jar for a month or so and will need to be able to soak up a fair bit of liquid. Stoning the cherries is not necessary but just be aware when you are using them at a later date that they have the stones in them. When I worked in pastry at St. John Bread and Wine we religiously never took the stones out of fruit when we baked with them, purely to leave the fruit in its own natural form. There is something quite nice about eating a cherry and popping the stone out of your mouth.

300g cherries
¼ cup fennel top flowers or fennel tops
10 black peppercorns
180ml water
250ml raw unfiltered apple cider vinegar
125g caster sugar
pinch of sea salt

1. Wash the cherries in cold water and remove the stalks. Use a bamboo skewer to prick each cherry a couple of times and put them in a sterilised jar that has cooled down. Add the fennel tops and peppercorns.

2. Put the water, vinegar, sugar and salt in a saucepan and bring to the boil. Simmer for 5 minutes, then turn off the heat and leave to cool for 5 minutes before pouring the liquid over the cherries and seal immediately.

3. Leave to pickle for two weeks before using. Once opened, keep in the fridge.

BLACK CHERRY & KIRSCH JAM

Makes 7 x 220g jars

A friend of mine once brought back a tray of cherries that she bought on the roadside in Kent and they were so luscious, verging on a dark purplish-black colour – they reminded me of Uma Thurman's nail colour in *Pulp Fiction*. This was before I had a cherry stoner and I remember sitting out in my garden manually stoning the fruit and my hands became stained with dark cherry juice. I never knew what variety they were, but I suspect they could have been a Kordia variety, known for producing the 'blackest' of all cherries with fruit larger than the average size. This recipe uses kirsch, a fruit brandy made from distilling cherries. This is a soft-set jam – cherries don't have high amounts of pectin so you may need to cook it for a little longer to try to thicken it.

1.8kg cherries
700g caster sugar
juice of 1 lemon
200g Green Apple Stock Jelly (see page 160)
100ml kirsch

1. First, stone your cherries, either by hand or using a cherry stoner. Once you've finished, run your fingers through the fruit to check whether you can feel any stones. Don't worry if you miss a few as once the jam starts cooking any stones will rise to the surface and you can scoop them out with a spoon.

2. Put the cherries in a heavy-based saucepan, set over a medium heat, cover with a lid and cook for 5 minutes or until the cherries become soft. Be careful not to let the juices evaporate as the point here is to release the juices.

3. Slowly add the sugar and then the lemon juice, jelly and kirsch and bring to the boil. Cook rapidly for 10 minutes or until the jam reaches setting point, 105°C/220°F on a sugar thermometer. Pour into warm sterilised jars and seal immediately. Store in a cool dark place.

BLACKCURRANT & ALMOND JAM

Makes 7 x 220g jars

Blackcurrants aren't for the faint-hearted. They produce an intense acidic jam that needs a friendly ingredient to soften it, one that won't be bullied by their flavour, something more textural like an almond. I like to add almonds as they add a more savoury texture with a nice bite. I don't recommend this as a toast jam because of its intensity but that is completely up to the jam-maker. It just feels a litte sharp for the early morning.

1.2kg blackcurrants (you can include the leaves if you have some)
700g caster sugar
200g whole almonds, roughly chopped
1 vanilla pod, cut in half lengthways and seeds scraped out
juice of 1 lemon

1. To prepare blackcurrants, gently wash them and remove any large stalks or brown leaves, but leave in any green leaves as they are very flavoursome and will add lots more depth to the jam.

2. Gently strain off any excess water and put the blackcurrants and any of their leaves (roughly torn) in a heavy-based saucepan with the scraped vanilla pod and seeds. Set over a low heat and cook until the fruit starts to break down, then add the sugar, almonds and lemon juice and slowly bring to the boil. Cook for about 8 minutes or until the jam reaches setting point, 105°C/220°F on a sugar thermometer. Because blackcurrants are high in pectin this jam doesn't take long to cook so keep an eye on it. Pour into warm sterilised jars and seal immediately. Store in a cool dark place.

TIPS
Acidic and tart blackcurrants go really well with anything creamy so I suggest pairing this with a thick ewes' milk yogurt for a quick pudding or using it at the bottom of a Bakewell tart served with Jersey cream.

I don't really like to combine fruit together in jams but if you feel that straight-up blackcurrant is a bit intense, try cooking with rhubarb, which will soften the flavour a little, using a proportion of half and half.

GREEN WALNUT LIQUEUR (NOCINO)
Makes 1-litre bottle

This sweet and sticky liqueur is traditionally made in northern Italy from unripe walnuts that have been picked at the start of summer when the green walnuts are soft and young and have a jelly-like centre. Left on the tree, these green walnuts will form into a hard brown walnut as the season ends. The lovely part about making this drink is the oxidisation process: as you cut the fresh walnuts, they start to discolour and turn your fingers yellow. Adding them to the jar with the other ingredients slowly turns the spirit brown then dark brown. I have read that traditionally you shouldn't drink nocino before 3rd November, which would mean it would be infusing for five months or so, but you could leave for much longer.

25 green walnuts
1 vanilla pod, cut in half lengthways
3 star anise
3 black cardamom pods
zest of 1 unwaxed orange and 1 unwaxed lemon
200g demerara sugar
750ml vodka

1. Slice the walnuts in half. If they are still very young you shouldn't have any problems in slicing them, but if they seem a little tough discard the firmer ones.

2. Put the walnuts in a 1.5-litre Kilner jar with a good clasp. Add the spices, citrus zest and sugar and pour over the vodka. The black cardamom will give a lovely smoky flavour.

3. Seal the jar tightly with the clasp and store in a cool dark place for four months. Every week or so, turn the jar upside down to give it a mix and help dissolve the sugar.

4. After four months, strain the liquid, discard the spices and walnuts, and decant into a sterilised bottle. Leave until 3rd November, then give it your first try – it will improve for at least a year.

> TIPS
> Serve as a quick and easy dessert poured over ice cream like an affogato.
>
> Drink neat after a long day.

PICKLED WATERMELON RIND

Makes 1 x 1 litre jar

What a shame to throw out the rind of a watermelon after you have eaten all the soft sweet crimson inner flesh. Like the ideology of eating nose-to-tail, I like to try and apply this no-waste philosophy to all the ingredients I use. You need to take off the green outer layer of the watermelon rind because it is really tough and won't break down in the vinegar brine. Use the firm white flesh that lies between the fruit and skin. And don't worry if you still have a little bit of pink flesh on the rind, this adds to the flavour and pretty appearance. I save the rind after I have eaten the flesh and keep it stored in the fridge until I have enough to make the pickle.

1kg watermelon rind
300ml raw unfiltered apple cider vinegar
250ml caster sugar
2 teaspoons sea salt
5 green cardamom pods
1 teaspoon brown mustard seeds
handful of basil stalks or fresh bay leaves

1. Cut the outer green skin from the watermelon and discard. Depending on how big your pieces are, you may find it easier to cut the rind into 5cm/2in squares and then peel the skin.

2. Put the white rind in a saucepan, cover with water and bring to the boil. Strain immediately and leave to cool.

3. Put the vinegar, sugar, salt, cardamom and mustard seeds in a large saucepan, set over a moderate heat and bring to a gentle simmer.

4. Add the cooled rind and basil stalks or bay leaves and simmer gently for 5 minutes. Remove from the heat and leave to cool.

5. Transfer all the ingredients to an airtight container and leave in the fridge overnight before using. The pickle will keep in the fridge for up to a month.

FIG LEAF SYRUP

Makes 1 x 750ml jar

There was a huge fig tree in our back garden in Melbourne, Australia when I was growing up, which meant I spent a lot of time swinging from and climbing it, not to mention eating the ripe fruit before the birds did. The tree hung over my cubby house, which I never used. Instead, I would hang out in the tree as it had large branches that were very comfortable and closer to the sunshine, away from the spiders in the cubby house. Now the scent of a fig tree reminds me of those hot summer days of my childhood. If you tear into a fig leaf you will notice a tropical green coconut flavour that gets even more intense when a hot liquid is poured over it.

8 fresh fig leaves
600g caster sugar
600ml water

1. When picking your fig leaves, try and cut as close to the leaf as possible as the stalk will produce a white sap that can make your hands itchy.

2. Tear up the leaves and put them in a sterilised 750ml jar that has cooled.

3. Put the sugar and water in a heavy-based saucepan. Set over a medium heat and bring to the boil and boil until it reaches 100°C/212°F on a sugar thermometer.

4. Remove from the heat, pour the hot syrup over the leaves and seal immediately – fig leaves are very hardy and need a hot extraction to get the best flavour. Leave in a cool dark place to infuse for two weeks before using.

TIPS
Try making a fig leaf aperitif with vodka by adding a dash of
Fig Leaf Syrup to soda water and lemon slices and the juice of
1 lemon.

Fig leaves can be used to infuse custards and ice creams or try
making a cordial with this syrup and freezing into ice-cube trays
like the Giant Hibiscus Flower Ice Cubes (see page 32).

REDCURRANT & VERJUICE JELLY

Makes 10 x 220g jars

Verjuice was introduced to me when I first started cooking in Australia, thanks to the much-celebrated cook Maggie Beer who started bottling it on a commercial basis. Verjuice is the juice of unfermented grapes and has the acidity of vinegar and the tartness of lemon juice but is much less astringent. I like to add it at the start of the cooking process so that it reduces with the redcurrant juice and becomes more intense.

1.4kg redcurrants
3.3 litres water
1.5kg caster sugar
250ml verjuice

1. Put the redcurrants and water in a heavy-based saucepan set over a medium heat. Bring to the boil, then reduce the heat to a simmer and cook for 20 minutes without mashing up the fruit too much as this will affect the clearness of the jelly.

2. Strain through a cheesecloth-lined colander set over a large bowl and leave overnight.

3. The following day, discard the pulp and measure the strained liquid – you should end up with about 2.3–2.5 litres of clear liquid.

4. Pour the liquid into a preserving pan and bring to the boil. Slowly add the sugar and verjuice and boil for about 25 minutes until setting point is reached. A good indication that it is ready is if you stir the boiling liquid with a wooden spoon and find that all the bubbles rise up and seem to overflow and the bubbles start to look more like foam.

5. Once setting point is reached, don't delay as it will start to set immediately. Pour quickly into a large jug, leave for 2 minutes and then skim off the top. (The top is where the bubbles will rise and start setting, if you skim this off you won't have any bubbles in the jelly.) Pour into warm sterilised jars and seal immediately. Store in a cool dark place.

RED GOOSEBERRY & ROSEMARY JAM

Makes 6 x 220g jars

Once the green gooseberries have been picked and summer is well underway, red gooseberries start appearing. These are much sweeter than the green ones and can be eaten raw or, more importantly, cooked into a luscious jam. I like to combine them with the woody hints of rosemary. At this time of year you may find yellow, white, red, purple or nearly black gooseberries. Some of the more readily available red varieties that I use are Whinham's Industry, Hinnomaki Red and Invicta.

1.25kg red gooseberries
2 sprigs of rosemary
100ml water
700g caster sugar
juice of 1 lemon

1. To prepare the gooseberries, wash them gently in cold water and top and tail them with a pair of scissors.

2. Put them in a preserving pan and add the rosemary and 100ml water. Set over a medium heat and cook until the berries start to break down and the rosemary releases its flavour.

3. Once the gooseberries are half cooked, slowly add the sugar and lemon juice and boil for 10 minutes or until the jam reaches setting point, 105°C/220°F on a sugar thermometer. (Gooseberries are high in pectin so this jam should produce a thick set jam. If you wish for it to be a little less set then cook it for 6–7 minutes.) Pour into warm sterilised jars and seal immediately. Store in a cool dark place.

DANDELION VINEGAR

Growing up, I didn't think much about dandelions apart from the soft fluffy head they create once the flower has gone to seed. I would religiously pick these in late summer and blow the tops off to make a wish. In fact, I still do this. The dandelion is one of the most underrated weeds on our planet – its health benefits are said to be some of the most important in herbal medicine. Try picking the greens in early summer before they start developing and become tough. You can use both the root and the green parts. Just ensure you pick these as far away from polluted areas as you can. You can make however much you like with this recipe, just make sure the jar is packed with the roots and leaves and totally covered in vinegar.

dandelion roots and leaves
raw unfiltered apple cider vinegar

1. Wash and scrub both the dandelion roots and leaves and cut into 5cm/2in pieces.

2. Put the roots and leaves in a sterilised jar and pour over enough vinegar to cover.

3. Seal the jar and leave in a cool dark place to infuse for eight weeks. Strain through cheesecloth and decant into sterilised bottles. Use the vinegar as you would any vinegar for your salad dressings.

TIP
The health benefits of drinking dandelion vinegar are extremely beneficial – try drinking a small glass of it before a meal. It can be a little intense so you can dilute it with a little cold water.

BOLD

JUICY

SMOKY

SPICY

BURNISHING

BLU

I S H

MULBERRIES AT HOGARTH'S HOUSE & GLENLYON

Forever chasing mulberries ... This seems to be me, or are they chasing me?

Every year in early summer I receive mulberry tree fan mail. It started over five years ago with the lovely Gentle Author, the pen name of a chronicler of life in the East End, who began documenting the mulberry trees around London and invited me to accompany him. Since then, I receive wonderful messages from many people all over the UK inviting me to come and pick the fruit from their trees, including the lovely couple who come into my shop every year telling me a friend has a HUGE mulberry tree – please come again next year and remind me where it is. I even have to try and beat James Lowe, head chef and owner at Lyle's restaurant and my former head chef at St. John Bread and Wine, to the mulberry tree as he is notorious for jumping high fences and taking them all before you can get to them! Perhaps the very fact that mulberries are hard to find and not in abundance makes them even more desirable. Their earthy rich port-like flavour is like no other berry I have tasted.

My favourable encounter with a mulberry tree was on a visit back to my parents in rural Victoria in Australia last year. I was having lunch with my mum in the local general store in Glenlyon, a small pretty town just out of Daylesford, when I noticed a few punnets of local, plump mulberries on the counter. I quickly snapped them up, treating them like little nuggets of gold, price not an issue in this instance as I would have done anything to get my hands on enough to make a batch of jam. In fact, I couldn't remember the last time I had enough to make jam with them.

After some local town investigative work, my dad helped me determine where the Glenlyon mulberries had come from. We set off to see if I would be able to get more at Adsum Farmhouse, a market garden set on three acres of volcanic soil, complete with an 80-year-old mulberry tree laden with fruit. This was by far the most impressive tree I had seen back home: it had so much fruit on it that I knew I would be able to make jam. I ended up ordering 2kg of fruit and we returned the following day to collect it. Thank you, trusty owners, for picking mulberries high up in that grand tree for me.

My Glenlyon bounty led to eight jars of jam, half of which remained with my mum in her larder so that she had some more memories of her long-lost daughter who lives on the other side of the world; one jar went to the fantastic chef at Du Fermier in Trentham, Victoria, Annie Smithers; the others I brought back with me to the UK as gifts to show off the wonderful fruit from my journey back home to Australia.

Another of my recent mulberry encounters was courtesy of the generous people at Hogarth's House in Chiswick, London. This was the country home of artist and engraver William Hogarth, which he bought in 1749. High brick walls still enclose the eighteenth-century house, though sadly it is now enveloped by roads that lead to the M4 and new-build housing. The development surrounding the walls is so vast and noisy I found it hard to imagine that this was once a country home.

Once you enter the small gate off the main road, you can see the the mulberry tree that has become just as famous as the house. Surprisingly, it is very quiet behind the gates and high walls and the wonderful old tree feels like an oasis surrounded by wild grass and flowers.

I received an email from an employee at Hogarth's House a few years back asking me if I would like to come and pick mulberries from their 300-year-old tree, and in return give them half the jam that I would make. As misfortune would have it, an intruder came and picked them all before I even had time to respond to the request, so my mulberry mission was put on hold until the following year. With the season being a good three weeks early, was I guaranteed a harvest?

I made the trip to the tree on a rainy late summer's day and, fortuitously, as I arrived the rain stopped. I carried my brightly coloured plastic Pound Shop tubs into the garden and checked in with reception to let them know that I had arrived, excited and hopeful. I then made my way to the tree, pausing for a moment as initially I couldn't see any berries, but on closer inspection I could see the dark purple gems hanging in the sunlight. This seems to apply when picking most fruit – your eye doesn't see much to begin with, but once you start picking the fruit they seem to appear everywhere!

A word of warning when picking mulberries: wear your darkest clothes as mulberries like to drip a dark red juicy liquid when you are picking them and you will end up with stained hands – but don't worry, it will wash off.

My day of picking mulberries at Hogarth's House produced only about 300g of fruit. I think I need to invest in a picking pole as sadly all the goodies were at the top of the tree away from stealing hands. These particular mulberries were used to infuse a bottle of vodka. I now have a hot-pink alcoholic drink to savour when I feel depressed about not being able to make mulberry jam. Perhaps next year I will get enough!

MULBERRY & CIDER VINEGAR JAM

Makes 7 x 220g jars

Mulberries are a tricky fruit for making jam as they contain very little pectin, which means you need the right balance of sugar and acid to help it set. Here I'm using apple cider vinegar. You'll never get a firm-set jam unless you want to add another fruit to help it along. I prefer not to cook this sacred fruit with any other ingredients apart from the basics as I want to keep the precious mulberry flavour as pure as possible. Try to look out for juicy, plump fruit as small dry mulberries are better suited for popping into some spirits to infuse.

1.5kg mulberries
900g sugar
200ml raw unfiltered apple cider vinegar

1. Put the mulberries in a preserving pan set over a low heat and cook for about 5 minutes so that they begin to release their juices. Be careful not to have the heat high as all the lovely juices will start evaporating – you want to release the juices here and soften the berries.

2. After 5 minutes of slowly cooking them, gradually add the sugar and stir until dissolved, then add the vinegar and bring to the boil. (I usually cook this a little longer than other berries as it needs a little help thickening.)

3. Bring to the boil and cook the jam for 10–12 minutes or until the jam reaches setting point, 105°C/220°F on a sugar thermometer. Keep an eye on the jam and ensure it doesn't start to stick as it will reduce quickly. If you feel it sticking, turn the heat right down, stir and then bring back to the boil. Pour into warm sterilised jars and seal immediately. Store in a cool dark place.

GREENGAGE & PECAN JAM

Makes 7 x 220g jars

One of my favourite fruit to make jam with is the superior greengage or, to be specific, Reine Claude. These pale green-yellowish round plums are a little smaller than more common plums and a little bit bigger than Mirabelles. Honeyed ripe greengages are sometimes referred to as the 'confectionery of fruit' so I like to pair them with something a little savoury like pecan nuts. This is the older brother to my Greengage & Fennel Pollen Jam, one of my first and very favourite jams.

1.6kg greengages, halved and stoned
150ml water
800g sugar
juice of 1 lemon
150g pecan halves

1. Put the greengages in a heavy-based saucepan with the water (so that they don't stick), set over a medium heat and cook for 5 minutes.

2. Once the plums start to break down, slowly add the sugar and lemon juice and bring to the boil.

3. Meanwhile, roughly chop the pecan into small pieces but try to keep them slightly chunky so that they add some texture to the finished jam.

4. Add the pecans to the pan and cook for 8 minutes or until the jam reaches setting point, 105°C/220°F on a sugar thermometer. Pour into warm sterilised jars and seal immediately. Store in a cool dark place.

TIP
Sadly greengages aren't available at most grocery shops but if you keep an eye out you should find some at farmers' markets or speciality grocers. Try and look out for Reine Claude, which is an early French variety, or Cambridge Gage, which tends to be a darker blue-green.

FIG & EARL GREY JAM

Makes 9 x 220g jars

This is hands down LBJ's most popular jam. The fig season varies from year to year and sometimes it can last right up until early winter, which makes for very happy customers. I often wonder what it is about this particular jam that drives people so crazy – could it be the delicate Earl Grey tea that I use, studded with cornflowers, or the savoury textures the fig seeds produce when eaten straight from the jar or with cheese? Either way, I'm now giving away the recipe so I'm hoping to spread the LBJ Fig & Earl Grey Jam love. Try to select the softest and ripest figs you can find; if they are hard it will be a struggle cooking them down so leave the figs for a few days at room temperature to help them ripen.

1.5kg ripe figs (I use Turkish figs)
10g loose Earl Grey tea leaves
  (with or without cornflowers)
1kg caster sugar
juice of 1 lemon

1. Slice the figs in half, place flat-side down on a board and cut into 5mm/¼in slices. Put all the fruit in a heavy-based saucepan with the tea leaves and set over a low heat for 5 minutes. The aim is to release the tea flavours alongside the natural fig juices.

2. Slowly add the sugar and lemon juice and stir until the sugar has dissolved. Turn the heat up to high and cook for about 10 minutes, checking every so often that the jam is not sticking, until it reaches setting point, 105°C/220°F on a sugar thermometer. Pour into warm sterilised jars and seal immediately. Store in a cool dark place.

TIP
Take the stalks off your figs and try to slice closer to the inner flesh as some people (I am one of them) are allergic to the white glue-like sap that comes out of the stalks. If your hands start to tingle then slice the figs wearing gloves.

TIP
Cocoa beans are the seed of the Theobroma cacao plant, a native of Central and South America. The fruit is picked and the beans are fermented before being dried, roasted and peeled. The nibs are just broken up pieces of the seeds. Buy them from a health food store, ready roasted and broken up.

BLACKBERRY & VINCOTTO JELLY

Makes 10 x 220g jars

Vincotto translates as 'cooked wine' in Italian and is a thick sweet molasses made from red wine grapes cooked down and reduced by about a fifth of their original volume. It's traditionally made in the Marche, Apulia, Veneto, Lombardy and Emilia Romagna regions in Italy and is used as a replacement for balsamic vinegar. The warmth of the concentrated grapes and blackberries creates a deep rich jelly that is perfect for cheese and cured meats. You will need the apples here to hold together the jelly.

1.5kg Bramley or Granny Smith apples
2.5 litres water
500g blackberries
1.5g caster sugar
4 tablespoons vincotto

1. Wash the apples and roughly chop into 5cm/2in pieces – no need to be too fussy as these will break down once soft. You want to cook all parts of the apple including the skin, core and pips as it all adds flavour and pectin. Put into a heavy-based saucepan with the water and blackberries and bring to the boil then turn down and simmer for 12–13 minutes. Try not to bash up the apples pieces as this will prevent the jelly from having a lovely crystal clear finish.

2. After 20 minutes, remove from the heat and strain through fine cheesecloth. Most jellies like to hang overnight to extract the maximum liquid but I tend to hang mine for 2–3 hours and find that's enough.

3. When you're ready to make your jelly, pour the strained liquid back into the clean heavy-based pan with the vincotto and set over a low heat. Slowly add the sugar and bring to the boil and cook vigorously for 20 minutes or until setting point is reached, 105°C/220°F on a sugar thermometer. Pour into warm sterilised jars and seal immediately. Store in a cool dark place.

BLACKBERRY & COCOA NIB JAM

Makes 5 x 220g jars

Chocolate and blackberries? Sounds good, doesn't it? When I was a pastry chef I remember once making a chocolate trifle with poached blackberries and the warmth of both the chocolate and berries had the same delicious effect as eating Black Forest gâteau. These flavours combined gave me the idea of cooking blackberries with pure, raw cocoa beans into a jam. I like to crush the cocoa beans a little before adding them so that the jam has a more intensely chocolate flavour.

1kg blackberries
600g caster sugar
45g cocoa nibs
juice of 1 lemon

1. First use a mortar and pestle to crush the cocoa nibs so that they start breaking down. Alternatively, you can roughly chop them on a board. I like to keep the nibs quite chunky but you can play around with the textures.

2. Put the blackberries in a heavy-based saucepan with the cocoa nibs, set over a gentle heat and cook for 5 minutes or until the juices start to run. Keep an eye on the pan as the cocoa can catch easily and burn so keep stirring.

3. Gradually add the sugar and lemon juice and turn the heat up and boil for 8 minutes or until the jam reaches setting point, 105°C/220°F on a sugar thermometer. Pour into warm sterilised jars and seal immediately. Store in a cool dark place.

LATE RASPBERRY & PURPLE BASIL JAM

Makes 5 x 220g jars

Raspberries soldier on. As the early plums start appearing and the days are getting shorter and cooler, the raspberries keep going, which is a huge bonus if you're hanging on to the jam season. I could never tire of having raspberry jam in the fridge, especially using the later ones which are a little tarter and are delicious, alongside some sugar. If you are lucky and have a greenhouse or can manage to create a little microclimate (like I have at the back of my shop), you may be able to grow some basil or in this instance purple basil, which has a more heady aroma than the green variety. You will need to prepare this jam the day before you intend to cook it.

1kg raspberries
600g caster sugar
½ cup purple basil leaves, torn into pieces
juice of 1 lemon

1. Combine the raspberries, sugar and basil leaves in a bowl, mix thoroughly and cover with a tea-towel. Leave to macerate overnight – this helps draw out the flavours of the basil.

2. The following day, put the macerated ingredients and the lemon juice in a heavy-based saucepan and set over a medium heat, stirring so that it doesn't catch. Bring to the boil and cook for 10 minutes or until the jam reaches setting point, 105°C/220°F on a sugar thermometer. Pour into warm sterilised jars and seal immediately. Store in a cool dark place.

TIP
Try using this jam to make jammy dodger biscuits. Make a simple shortbread biscuit base, roll and cut out with a small circular cutter and keep half for a flat-bottom base, and cut out a small hole in the other half. Bake separately and then sandwich together with some jam.

TOMATO JAM

'GREEK HOLIDAYS'
Makes 5 x 220g jars

I was first served tomato jam in Greece alongside a sheeps' milk cheese and fluffy white bread with a crust. The flavours that stood out most were cinnamon and the sharpness of the vinegar. With this recipe you need to be generous with the tomatoes as they release a lot of liquid and will quickly reduce down, leaving an overly sweet jam. I can't really recommend a specific tomato here as I hope you've grown so many that you just use up what you have but try to look for juicy and fragrant tomatoes that actually taste of something – these days they can seem hard to find. I find that this recipe needs a much longer cooking time than other jam recipes but you need be careful that it doesn't end up too sweet.

1.6kg tomatoes
2 cinnamon sticks
650g caster sugar
200ml apple cider vinegar (preferably one that has a mother in it)

1. To prepare the tomatoes, bring a large saucepan of water to the boil and have a large bowl of iced water ready. Use a small knife to carve a little cross into the base of each tomato. Drop them into the boiling water for 1 minute, then remove using a slotted spoon or tongs and immediately place in the iced water. You may need to do this in a few batches, depending on the size of the saucepan. Leave the tomatoes to completely cool in the iced water for 5 minutes then drain. Starting from the bottom of the tomato, you will now be able to peel the skins off the flesh.

2. Slice each skinned tomato into halves and then into quarters and put in a heavy-based saucepan with the cinnamon and cook for about 10 minutes, until the tomatoes start to break down.

3. Slowly add the sugar and vinegar and bring to the boil. Cook for 20 minutes or until the jam reaches setting point, 105°C/220°F on a sugar thermometer. Pour into warm sterilised jars and seal immediately. Store in a cool dark place.

> TIP
> Another way to peel tomatoes is to halve them horizontally and place, cut-side down, in a roasting tin and slow-roast them in an oven preheated to 130°C/250°F/gas mark ½ for 30–40 minutes. Don't add any oil as this will give the jam an oily finish on top. Peel off the skins and cook as above.

PLUM & TOMATO LEAF JAM

Makes 5 x 220g jars

This is a very versatile recipe that calls for a more common plum variety that you would find in your local grocer like Dalmassine, Victoria or Lancelot. It also requires something that I hope most people will be able to get hold of: tomato leaves. You may know someone who grows tomatoes and won't mind giving you some of their cuttings when they prune their plants.

1kg Dalmassine plums, halved and stoned
100ml water
½ cup torn-up tomato leaves and stems
600g caster sugar
juice of 1 lemon

1. Put the plums in a heavy-based saucepan with the water and tomato leaves and stems, set over a medium heat and cook for 5 minutes or until the fruit is soft.

2. Once the plums start to break down, slowly add the sugar and lemon juice and bring to the boil. Cook for 10 minutes or until the jam reaches setting point, 105°C/220°F on a sugar thermometer. You may choose to take out some of the stalks as they might have a woody texture whereas the leaves will be softer and easier to eat. Pour into warm sterilised jars and seal immediately. Store in a cool dark place.

TIP
For a more intense tomato flavour, try placing your torn-up tomato leaves in the sugar and leave for a few days. Once the leaves have been picked, either cook with them straight away or pop into the sugar as they lose their flavour and scent quickly.

COBNUT & QUETSCHE PLUM MINCEMEAT

Makes 6 x 500ml jars

This is my take on the mincemeat that I used to make under my boss Justin Gellatly at St. John Restaurant. I have added fresh plums to make it less dried fruit heavy and soften the texture, and cobnuts for soft crunch. The secret to this recipe is cooking it slowly so that the suet doesn't split, and stirring it as it cools to help it bind together. If you can't find Quetsche plums, use Victoria plums, which have a good amount of flesh. Whatever you use, select larger plums to make the task of stoning them easier. Make this a few months in advance of Christmas and feed it a few times with brandy to help the flavour become punchy. I make mine with vegetarian suet but you can always use beef suet.

800g Quetsche plums (juicy ones), halved and stoned
800g Bramley or Granny Smith apples
120g cobnuts (shelled weight)
350g vegetarian suet
300g sultanas
300g raisins
250g dried figs, chopped
300g currants

1kg light brown sugar
zest and juice of 2 unwaxed lemons
zest and juice of 2 unwaxed oranges
2 teaspoons ground cinnamon
2 teaspoons ground nutmeg
2 teaspoons ground cardamom
2 teaspoons mixed spice
300ml brandy, plus extra for feeding

1. Bear in mind that the mincemeat is destined for a pie so chopping the fruit, and especially the apples, into small pieces is the most helpful – the plums will break down more easily so you can be a little more rough with them. Slice each halved plum into quarters and core and cut the apples into 1cm/½in cubes. Roughly chop the cobnuts.

2. Put the prepared fruit, cobnuts, suet, dried fruit, sugar, citrus zest and juice and spices in a large bowl and mix thoroughly. Cover the bowl with a tea-towel and leave overnight so the mixture starts to break down and steep.

3. The following day, preheat the oven to 120°C/250°F/gas mark ½. Tip the mincemeat into a deep roasting pan (depending on the oven size you may need to use two pans). Cook in the oven for 4 hours, stirring every 30 minutes. Once cooked, remove from the oven, pour over the brandy and stir through. Leave at room temperature until it completely cools, stirring occasionally so that when it starts cooling the fat from the suet binds the mix. If you leave it without stirring while cooling it will begin to split and won't bind together nicely.

4. Once cooled, transfer the mincemeat to six sterilised jars (ones that have a wide rim), cover with a piece of parchment paper, seal with a lid and leave in a cool dark place. After four weeks, distribute 50ml brandy between the jars and gently stir through the top of the mix before replacing the paper and lid. Repeat every four weeks until you are ready to use the mincemeat.

TIPS
If you prefer a smoother jam, try chopping up the skins or putting them in a blender.

You can also boil the grapes with some crab apples as you would the Rowanberry Jelly (see page 138), replacing the rowanberries with the grapes and straining through cheesecloth, then cook with the sugar. You will become a jelly expert after reading this book.

UVA FRAGOLA JAM
'STRAWBERRY GRAPES'
Makes 6 x 220g jars

When I first tasted these dark, strong-scented grapes from Piedmont in north Italy I was instantly transported back to tasting American grape bubblegum as a kid. I had a pen pal in the US and we used to write to each other monthly and swap sweets via letters. I wasn't really allowed many sweets as a child so perhaps this was a clever way of getting around it. In return, I used to send her 'fags', which were musk sticks – a classic sweet in Australia – resembling cigarettes; we loved those. The skins of Uva Fragola grapes peel off really easily and the jelly-like flesh is perfect for jams and jellies. Allow some time to prepare them, but it's well worth the effort and even quite meditative.

1.4kg Uva Fragola grapes (or you could use Concord grapes)
400g caster sugar
200g Green Apple Stock Jelly (see page 160) or any other
  jelly you can spare
juice of 1 lemon

1. Set yourself up with a large bowl for the peeled grapes and juices and another for the skins. Remove the grapes from the stalks. Individually peel the skins off each grape, working over a bowl so that you collect as much of the juice as possible. Set aside the skins in the second bowl.

2. Put the grapes and all the juice in a heavy-based saucepan, set over a medium heat and gently simmer for 10 minutes or until they have softened, being careful not to heat the liquid too much so that it evaporates.

3. Remove from the heat and pass the mixture through a mouli, the mouli will catch the seeds. You should end up with about a litre of grape flesh pulp and 900g of skins that you already set aside.

4. Put the pulp and skins in a the heavy-based saucepan, set over a medium heat and cook for 10 minutes or until the skins start breaking down. Slowly add the sugar, jelly and lemon juice. Bring to the boil and cook for 12 minutes or until the jam reaches setting point, 105°C/220°F on a sugar thermometer. Pour into warm sterilised jars and seal immediately. Store in a cool dark place.

MIRABELLE PLUM & STICKY TOKAY JAM
'FIREWORK JAM'
Makes 7 x 220g jars

The red flecks on small yellow Mirabelle plums are a pretty indication that you have found the Rolls-Royce of the plum world. These sweet little honey-tasting stone fruit are full of flavour and are traditionally used in France for jam-making. They don't have a long season – only about six weeks. The French love them so much that in the north eastern city of Metz they annually hold a fortnight-long Mirabelle festival that includes a firework display. This makes me think we should be holding more festivals celebrating fruit and seasonality, wherever we are in the world.

1.5kg Mirabelle plums
700g caster sugar
125ml Tokay wine
juice of 1 lemon

1. This jam takes a bit of time to prepare as you want to remove the stones from the little plums. If you are restricted for time, it's fine to stone them all and keep the flesh in the fridge until you are ready to make the jam, just squeeze over some lemon juice to stop them from discolouring.

2. Put the plums in a heavy-based saucepan, set over over a medium heat and cook the fruit until they start to release their juices – about 5 minutes.

3. Slowly add the sugar, Tokay wine and lemon juice and bring to the boil. Boil for 10 minutes or until the jam reaches setting point, 105°C/220°F on a sugar thermometer. Keep an eye on the jam and if it starts to catch, turn down the heat, stir and then bring back up to the boil. Pour into warm sterilised jars and seal immediately. Store in a cool dark place.

> TIP
> Tokay is a sweet white wine from the Tokaj wine region in Hungary. If you can't find Tokay wine then try another sweet wine – say an Alsace Muscat or a pink moscato from Italy.

BLOOD NECTARINE & SEA SALT JAM

Makes 7 x 220g jars

Nectavigne® is the branded name of a type of blood-red nectarine created by a French fruit breeder by crossing the nectarine with the pêche de vigne (see page 70). These nectarines are available up until the end of September and are just as exciting as their sister stone fruit, the pêche de vigne. These red-fleshed nectarines are super sweet, juicy and tangy with smooth skin, just like any other nectarine. As with all other stone fruit, ensure you use ones that are as soft as possible otherwise it will be difficult to cook them down with the sugar and you will end up with a jam with hard pieces of fruit.

1.6kg blood nectarines (about 10 nectarines), halved and stoned
100ml water
800g caster sugar
juice of 1 lemon
1 teaspoon sea salt flakes

1. Cut each nectarine half lengthways into quarters and then dice into 2cm/¾in cubes and put in a heavy-based saucepan with the water. Set over a medium heat and cook for 10 minutes. It might help to cover the pan with a lid to speed up the cooking process and let the fruit steam a little and break down more easily.

2. Once the fruit is soft, add the sugar, lemon juice and salt and cook for a further 10 minutes or until the jam reaches setting point, 105°C/220°F on a sugar thermometer. Leave to rest for 5 minutes to distribute the pieces of fruit before pouring into warm sterilised jars and sealing immediately. Store in a cool dark place.

ROASTED YELLOW PEACH & FENNEL JAM

Makes 10 x 220g jars

Have you ever roasted peaches with fennel tops? They taste delicious. I like to break up the fennel stalks and place the peaches on top with some caster sugar and then slow-roast them for an hour, keeping them in my fridge to use for an emergency porridge topping or to serve with yogurt and granola. Unlike poaching peaches in lots of liquid, this is a nice way of gently cooking them so that they caramelise and don't become watery.

2 large fennel bulbs with stalks (green fronds reserved), sliced vertically into long flat pieces
2kg yellow peaches, halved and stoned
150g demerara sugar
900g caster sugar
juice of 1 lemon

1. Preheat the oven to 130°C/250°F/gas mark ½.

2. Put the fennel slices in an ovenproof dish in a single layer and rest the peach halves on them, cut side up. Sprinkle with the demerara sugar and roast in the oven for about 1 hour or until the peaches are cooked and started to colour. Remove from the oven and leave to slightly cool.

3. Transfer the peaches, including the skins and juices (discarding the fennel pieces), to a heavy-based saucepan and set over a low heat. Tear up any of the green fennel fronds and scatter over the peaches. Add the caster sugar and lemon juice and cook for 10 minutes or until the jam reaches setting point, 105°C/220°F on a sugar thermometer. Pour into warm sterilised jars and seal immediately. Store in a cool dark place.

'LOVE IT.'

TIP
Try slow-roasting other stone fruit, such as nectarines and
plums, but ensure they are ripe enough or they won't
cook properly and release their tasty juices.

PICKLED ELDERBERRIES
THE GENEROUS ELDER TREE
Makes 2 x 500ml jars

Towards the end of summer, you will notice small purple berries forming – almost reminiscent of peppercorns in their early stages. These are another edible crop from the generous elder tree and a sign that the seasons are changing. The sour-tasting berries are perfect for making sauces and adding to jellies for colour and tartness. Traditionally served alongside game birds, elderberries are also used for preserving and as a natural dye. The flavour is concentrated and, for making jam or jelly, it's best to use elderberries with another autumnal fruit like apples and quinces to balance out the flavour. You can also pickle them and serve them over roasted game meats or chicken.

1.25kg elderberries with stalks
1 litre raw unfiltered apple cider vinegar
200g demerara sugar
200g caster sugar
3 fresh bay leaves
5 star anise

1. Picking elderberries off their stalks is a little time consuming so ensure you allow enough time to do this. Individually pick off all the berries into a bowl (using a fork makes this easier).

2. Put the vinegar, sugars, bay leaves and star anise in a stainless-steel saucepan, bring to the boil, reduce the heat to a simmer for 5 minutes, then turn off the heat and rest for a further 5 minutes.

3. Distribute the berries equally between two sterilised jars. Pour over the warm pickling liquid and seal immediately. These will keep in a cool dark place for up to six months but, once open, keep refrigerated.

ELDERBERRY & POMEGRANATE MOLASSES SYRUP
Makes 1 x 1 litre bottle

You need to be quick getting to the elderberries before the birds do and, depending on the weather, the ripe berries drop off easily – most of mine came off this year with the rain. So when you see a good tree, pick as many as you can and freeze them in small bags or make a big batch of this syrup. Try to look out for elder trees that are away from roadsides – head towards rural spots where the air is cleaner.

700g elderberries
1.2 litres water
1kg caster sugar
150ml pomegranate molasses

1. Pick the elderberries from the stems (using a fork makes it easier).

2. Put them in a large saucepan, add the water and bring to the boil. Once boiling, reduce the heat to a gentle simmer and cook for 15 minutes, using a wooden spoon to gently squash the berries.

3. Remove from the heat, pass the mixture through a fine sieve and return the liquid (you should have approx. 1.2 litres of liquid) to a clean saucepan with the sugar and pomegranate molasses.

4. Bring back to the boil and gently simmer for a further 25 minutes or until a light syrup is formed. Pour into warm sterilised bottles and cap immediately. Unopened, this will keep for up to six months in a cool dark place; thereafter keep refrigerated.

TIP
Once you have finished using the pickled berries, don't discard the liquid as it will still be really fragrant – instead use it for flavouring new jams, jellies or even toss through some vegetables before roasting them for flavour.

ROBUST

AMBER

SPIKY

THORNY

BRISTLING

BA

SEA
BUCKTHORN

Willow Walker has been picking sea buckthorn on the east coast of Scotland for the past 8 years. She chanced upon the wild spiny bushes that cover the dunes and was so taken by their mesmerising shades of orange, green and silver and the tart, sherbet-like berries that she set up a sea buckthorn business called Wild and Scottish, creating a line of hand-produced bottled juice. She is constantly amazed by this woody shrub that is capable of providing so many different things – food, medicine and shelter.

This deciduous shrub, native to Central Asia and parts of Europe, including coastal habitats of east England, has become widely naturalised on parts of the British coastline. Sea buckthorn was planted around certain coasts to control manmade and natural erosion that stripped the sand dunes of their vegetation. It rapidly spread and threatened to take over some areas, prompting many councils to dig it out and burn it off in a bid to control it. As a result, birds were unable to feed on the nutritious orange berries during the winter months or use the branches as roosts. More open-minded councils, however, come to sustainable agreements with people like Willow who pick certain quantities to help to maintain the crops. After 8 years working together, Willow and the local authority are both confident that the system they have created works well and is beneficial for the wildlife and native plants in the areas Willow harvests.

The first of the buckthorn berries appear in early autumn and cover most of the female plants, whereas the male plants don't produce any fruit. I noticed when I went picking with Willow that some of the female plants varied with the amounts of fruit and she explained to me that every year they differ, sometimes producing an abundance and the following year only a small amount. I wondered whether this is like the apple tree variety in my back garden that alternates every year, either producing fruit or not. I like to think of it having a rest from the previous year when it was laden with fruit and taking the time to build up energy to produce another crop.

Willow doesn't start picking the berries until October and continues to work until February. She likes to wait until the first few frosts have settled in and the berries have slowly started to soften or blet. Dressed in her trusty wet-weather gear from head to toe, including fisherman's thick rubber gloves, Willow harvests these bright berries. Instead of picking individual berries or cutting off long branches, she squeezes whole bunches of

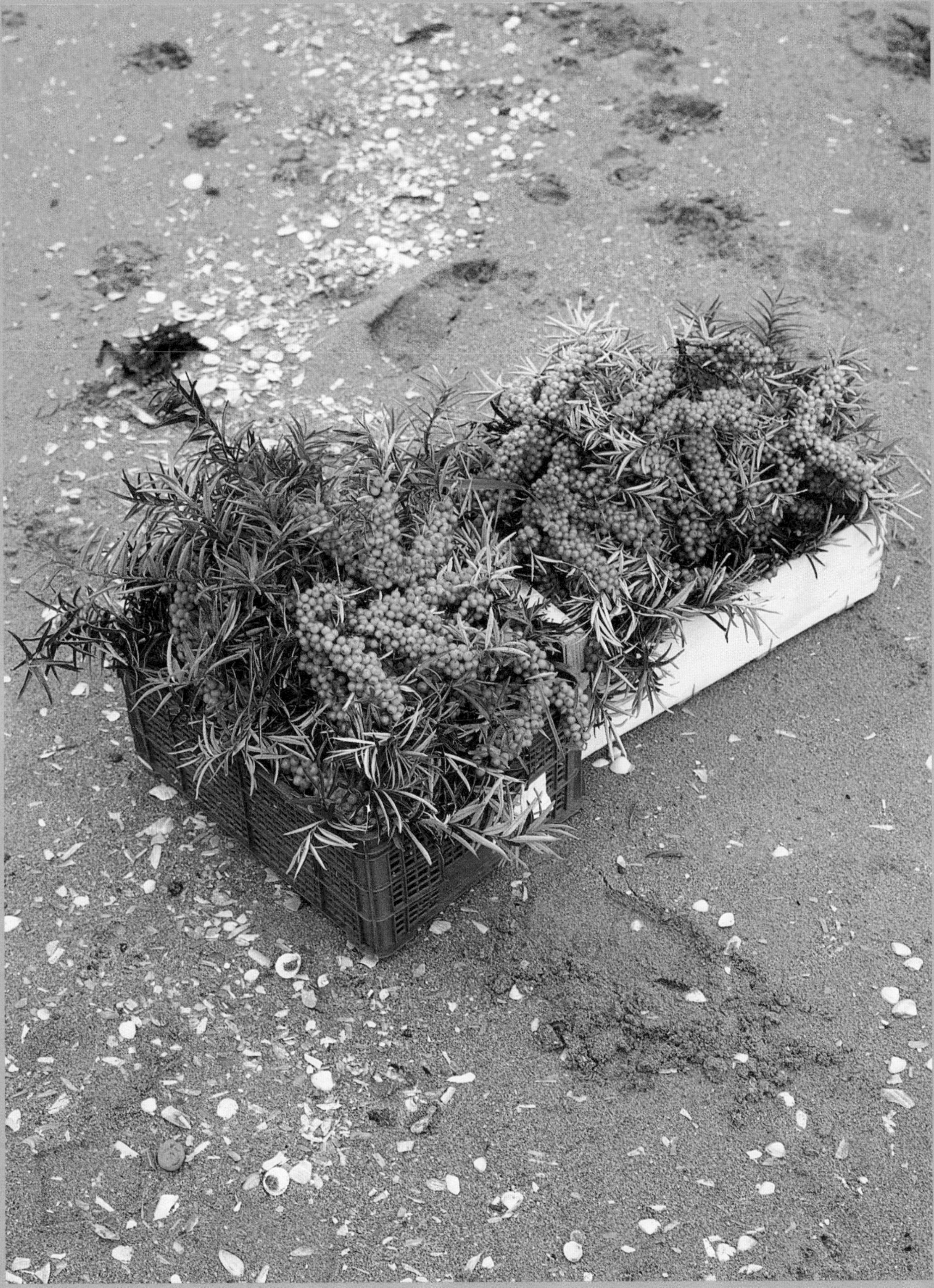

berries over a bucket and lets them fall naturally into it along with all the juices. She has to be careful once the bushes have begun to lose their leaves because the thorns on the bare twigs are extremely painful.

After a full day of collecting berries, Willow returns to her kitchen and starts processing them into her bottled juice. Sea buckthorn berries ferment quite quickly so it is important for her to preserve them as soon as possible. She also explained to me that, magically, her large stainless-steel pot holds exactly one batch of her recipe and, once bottled, fits perfectly into her recycled crates without any left over. I too find this extremely rewarding when I make jam and I fill the jars perfectly to the rim without any wasted.

Sea buckthorn berries contain up to 15 times more vitamin C than oranges and are full of vitamin E, omega oils, antioxidants, carotenes, flavonoids and many essential minerals. No wonder sea buckthorn has been attracting worldwide interest with its adaptogenic properties, which help us to adapt to stress, and varied uses in treating health problems. The shrub has also been a topic of research in some countries, such as India, where sea buckthorn has been introduced to the Ladakh region in the Himalayas and used for greening the mountain terrains. It is thought that developing the cultivation of sea buckthorn in this area alone could transform the local economy, following the example of China who is the largest producer of sea buckthorn products.

I've been using sea buckthorn since working at St. John Bread and Wine as our local forager would bring us in crates of it in late September and we would cook the berries into jellies, mainly to serve with game meats. At the start of the season, I have always found it easier to freeze the young whole twigs overnight and then pop off the frozen berries and avoid pricking my fingers on the thorns. Later in the season, once the berries have softened on the leafless branches and are easier to pull off, just ensure you have the right clothes on as it can get messy.

SEA BUCKTHORN JELLY

Makes 6 x 220g jars

Don't worry if you can't find any sea buckthorn bushes, this recipe will work well with bottled juice, which you can buy online, but using fresh ingredients is better because by using the whole fruit the pectin in the skins helps to provide a firmer texture that you won't get from juice alone. This is why I include apples in this jelly recipe as they act as the holding agent. I recommend keeping berries on their stalks in the freezer and take out as needed.

400g sea buckthorn berries (or 400ml sea buckthorn juice)
1.5kg Bramley apples, roughly chopped into 5cm/2in pieces
  (including skins and cores)
2.5 litres water
1.3kg caster sugar
juice of 1 lemon

1. If you have frozen stalks of sea buckthorn in your freezer, take out about 500g and very carefully pop off all the berries into a bowl. Don't be too fussy about the leaves and a few stalks going in as this will be passed through cheesecloth once it is cooked. You want about 400g frozen berries.

2. Put the berries (or juice) in a heavy-based saucepan with the apples and water. Bring to the boil, reduce the heat to a gentle simmer and cook for 12–13 minutes, until everything is really soft. Don't break up the fruit as this will make a cloudy jelly.

3. Strain the pulp through a cheesecloth-lined sieve set over a large bowl. Leave for 2 hours to allow the juice to drip through.

4. Once you have collected your juice (about 2 litres), pour it into a clean heavy-based saucepan and set over a medium heat. Cook for 3 minutes, then slowly add the sugar and lemon juice, bring to a rolling boil and cook 20 minutes or until the jelly reaches setting, 105°C/220°F on a sugar thermometer. Pour into warm sterilised jars and seal immediately. Store in a cool dark place.

TIPS
Be very careful when taking the frozen berries off the stalks because, like sloes, they have sharp thorns and can be painful.

For me, sea buckthorn tastes tart, fruity and passionfruit-like. The acidic berries can be infused in some cider vinegar for salad dressings or in a cup of water as a daily tonic.

QUINCE & ROSEWATER JAM

Κυδώνι Κμσώνί

Makes 7 x 220g jars

Every year I holiday at the same house in Greece with a lovely generous couple who have self-contained apartments connected to their family home. It was Olympia who introduced me to her version of *Κυδώνι Κμσώνί*, which translates as quince preserve. The longer you cook quinces the better the colour will be, so adding more water at the start gives the fruit much more room to cook down slowly and develop that pink blush.

1.5kg quinces (3 large ones)
2 litres water
1kg caster sugar
juice of 1 lemon
3 tablespoons rosewater

1. Wipe away any fur on the skin of the quinces. Peel, cut into halves and then quarters and remove the cores. Slice these long fingers in half lengthways. (I prefer a chunkier jam so I chop into 2cm/¾in cubes or you can try grating the fruit or slicing it thinly into discs.)

2. Choose a saucepan with high sides as if it's too shallow the liquid will evaporate quickly and not colour. Put the quince in your pan and add the water. Bring to the boil, then reduce the heat to a simmer and cook until the flesh is tender, about 20–25 minutes.

3. Add the sugar and lemon juice and bring back to the boil. Boil for 20 minutes and then reduce the heat to a gentle simmer and cook for a further 40 minutes, stirring every so often to check that it is not catching. It should be a really lovely ruby colour when you are ready to take it off the heat. Pour in the rosewater and stir through. Be careful, it may bubble a little as the jam is very hot. Leave to rest for 5 minutes and then pour into warm sterilised jars and seal immediately. Store in a cool dark place.

MARJORIE'S SEEDLING & JASMINE TEA JAM

Makes 7 x 220g jars

Marjorie's Seedling is a late autumn plum that is much better for cooking than as a table plum because it is less juicy than other varieties. Far better to use Marjorie's Seedlings in crumbles, ice creams, or poached and in jams. You will need to use ripe plums and gently cook them down with some water so that they soften nicely before you add the sugar, otherwise you will have hard bits of fruit in your jam. Try to buy a premium loose tea that is 100 per cent from its origin – many loose teas can be mixed with cheaper leaves and don't have the quality and flavour.

1.5kg ripe Marjorie's Seedling plums,
   halved and stoned
250ml water
3 teaspoons loose jasmine tea leaves
600g caster sugar
200g demerara sugar
juice of 1 lemon

1. Put the plums in a heavy-based saucepan with the water and tea leaves, set over a medium heat and cook the plums until they are completely soft. (If you are finding it difficult to cook down the fruit, put a lid on the pan to help to steam the plums. Unripe fruit just won't break down.)

2. Once the plums are soft, add the sugars and lemon juice and bring to the boil. Cook for 10 minutes or until the jam reaches setting point, 105°C/220°F on a sugar thermometer. Pour into warm sterilised jars and seal immediately. Store in a cool dark place.

TIP
If you aren't keen on having tea leaves in your jams then you can wrap the loose tea in some cheesecloth and tie with some string, then add to the pan with the plums and water.

ROSEHIP & LEMON VERBENA SYRUP
Makes 3 x 500ml bottles

As the leaves drop you will start noticing many rose bush skeletons with nothing left but little red fruit, or hips, the last edible part of the plant. You can use rosehips for many things including syrups, teas and even ketchup, and they are an excellent source of vitamin C. I like to dehydrate mine and grind them into a power to sprinkle on warming bowls of porridge in winter. You will need to sieve the powder to remove any of the hairy bits that are inside the rosehip as they can be extremely irritating to eat.

500g wild rosehips, washed and roughly chopped
1 cup fresh lemon verbena leaves, torn into pieces
2.2 litres water
100ml white wine vinegar
800ml demerera sugar

1. Put the rosehips in a large saucepan with 1.2 litres of the water, the vinegar and lemon verbena leaves. Bring to the boil and cook for 5 minutes. Remove from the heat and leave to infuse for 20 minutes.

2. Strain through a cheesecloth-lined sieve set over a large bowl to collect the juice and leave for 1 hour – don't be tempted to push the pulp though as this will just make the syrup cloudy.

3. Return the pulp to the saucepan with the remaining water. Bring to the boil and cook for 5 minutes, then remove from the heat and leave for a further 20 minutes. Strain through the cheesecloth-lined sieve a second time – you should end up with about 1.8 litres of liquid.

4. Pour the liquid into a clean saucepan and add the sugar. Bring to the boil and cook rapidly for 15 minutes, skimming off any impurities or foam that rise to the surface.

5. Remove from the heat and leave to rest for 5 minutes before pouring into warm sterilised bottles and sealing immediately. Store in a cool dark place.

TIP
This syrup will keep for three months, after that pop into the fridge and it will keep for a further three months.

TIP
You can slow-roast whole bletted medlars in a roasting pan with some sugar and vanilla. Add a small amount of water (about 100ml) to the pan and cover with foil to help them steam. You won't get much flesh out of each one so be generous when serving.

MEDLAR & ROSEMARY JELLY
Makes 7 x 220g jars

Medlars are one of those strange fruit that most people know about but don't really know what to do with them – you can't simply pick them from the tree and eat them raw. Medlars, like quince, are what I like to call slow-burning fruit, ones that take time to prepare and cook. Once I have picked them I usually leave them in my shop as a display because they look so pretty and offer a nice talking point. They also need to be left to become completely soft, or bletted, before you can boil them up to make a jelly. This may take a few weeks or a month depending on the temperature. My shop stays very cool so they tend to take around a month. Spread them out flat on a tray, rather than piled on top of each other, so that they don't go mouldy.

I am lucky to have a medlar tree near my house but you have to be quick: last year when I went to collect some the entire bottom half of the tree had no fruit left but the top half (out of arm's reach) was full. It made for a pretty frustrating picture.

1.2kg medlars, bletted
2 Bramley or Granny Smith apples, roughly chopped (including skins and cores)
2.5 litres water
2 sprigs of rosemary
800g caster sugar
juice of 1 lemon

1. Slice the medlars in half and place in a saucepan with the apples and water and bring to the boil. Reduce the heat to a simmer and cook for 25 minutes. (Don't cook this on a heavy boil as it will break up all the fruit and make a cloudy jelly, so keep it on a medium heat.) You may need to prod some of the harder medlars with a wooden spoon to help them break down, but don't mash them up as this will also make the jelly cloudy.

2. Remove from the heat, leave to rest for 5 minutes and then strain the fruit through a cheesecloth-lined sieve set over a large bowl and leave for 2 hours to hang.

3. Measure the strained liquid – you should end up with about 1.5 litres liquid. Return it to the cleaned saucepan and add the rosemary. Bring to the boil, reduce the heat and add the sugar, stirring to dissolve, and the lemon juice. Bring back to a rolling boil and cook rapidy for 20 minutes or until the jam reaches setting point, 105°C/220°F on a sugar thermometer.

4. Remove from the heat and pull out the long stems from the rosemary but leave in the small leaves. Pour into warm sterilised jars and seal immediately. Store in a cool dark place.

POACHED RUBY QUINCES

Makes 2 x 1 litre jars

Quinces like a lot of sugar when they are cooking and this helps them to become a dark, rich ruby colour. I like to cook them as slowly as possible and for a long time; starting early evening is a good time as you can turn off the oven and let them cool overnight, they will continue to gently cook for a few more hours and soak up more of the rich juices. It's best to use a flameproof heavy-based cast iron pot with a lid and you need to ensure that the quinces are completely covered in liquid and have enough room to swim a little. However, don't fill the pot more than three-quarters full or it will overflow and the poaching liquid will cook into caramel on the bottom of your oven.

300g demerara sugar
500g caster sugar
800ml water
500ml verjuice
3 fresh bay leaves
1.5kg quince

1. Preheat the oven to 180°C/350°F/gas mark 4.

2. Put the sugars, water, verjuice and bay leaves in your flameproof heavy-based casserole set over a medium heat and stir to dissolve sugar.

3. Some quinces have a little fur on the skin so give them a rinse under warm water and wipe this away. Peel the quinces and depending on their sizes cut into quarters leaving the cores intact.

4. Remove the pot from the heat and place the quince pieces into the warm liquid. If you feel that there is too much liquid in the pot (more than three-quarters full) then take a little out and set aside – you can always add it back. Cut a circle of parchment paper and cover the top of the liquid and place the lid on top, keeping it slightly ajar so that some of the steam can escape.

5. Put the pot in the oven, turn the temperature down to 120°C/250°F/gas mark ½ and cook for 4 hours. Turn off the heat and leave the quinces in the oven overnight.

6. The following day, transfer the quinces and the cooking liquid to sterilised jars and seal. Store in the fridge and use within four weeks.

TIPS
I used larger quinces in this recipe but you may come
across smaller varieties that you can cook in the same way
but just for a shorter cooking time.

You can also cook the quince in a deep baking dish if you
have one large enough to hold all the liquid. Cover with
parchment paper and foil.

CRAB APPLE & VERJUICE JELLY

Makes 7 x 220g jars

Crab apples are a crop of miniature apples that you find growing wild in hedgerows and woodlands. There are so many different cultivars that you might get a little confused, but generally speaking they are all good to use and contain a healthy amount of pectin. Some are the size of damsons (tiny), whereas others can be as big as a golf ball. They have a neutral apple flavour so you can play around with this recipe and experiment with other complementary herbs, spices or alcohol. Just be careful when adding extra liquid that you make up for it with a little bit more sugar to balance it out.

1kg crab apples
2.5 litres water
800g caster sugar
300ml verjuice

1. Give the crab apples a good clean in cold running water. If you are using really small ones, keep them whole and don't worry about discarding any leaves and twigs. If you are using larger crab apples, slice them in half to help them to cook a bit quicker.

2. Put the crab apples in a heavy-based saucepan, add the water and bring to the boil. Turn down to a medium heat and cook for 15 minutes, remove from the heat and leave to rest for a couple of minutes.

3. Strain the pulp though a cheesecloth-lined sieve set over a large bowl and leave for 2 hours to get as much liquid out at possible. Don't be tempted to squeeze the bag as pushing the liquid through will make it cloudy.

4. Measure the strained liquid – you should have about 1.5 litres – pour into a clean saucepan, add the verjuice and set over a medium heat. Slowly add the sugar, bring to a rolling boil and cook for 20 minutes or until the jelly reaches setting point, 105°C/220°F on a sugar thermometer. Pour into warm sterilised jars and seal immediately. Store in a cool dark place.

ROWANBERRY JELLY

Makes 7 x 220g jars

Be quick: the birds are hungry in late autumn, and they love rowanberries, the fruit of a small deciduous tree or shrub that can grow up to 20 metres tall. The clusters of berries are usually red or orange or can be pink, yellow or white in some Asian species. The fruit taste very bitter and are not to be eaten raw. They contain virtually no pectin, which is why you need to cook them with high-pectin apples, just like the Sea Buckthorn Jelly (see page 128). Rowanberry jelly is traditionally served alongside game birds like grouse and partridge, and a few tablespoons of the jelly added to the juices in the bottom of your pan after roasting a bird will create a tasty sauce.

1kg crab apples or Bramley apples, roughly
   chopped, (including skinds and cores)
500g rowanberries
3 litres water
1kg caster sugar

1. Wash the apples and rowanberries. If you're using small crab apples you don't need to chop them.

2. Put the fruit in a heavy-based saucepan, along with any leaves and twigs from the rowanberries; don't pick through it as it will be strained.

3. Pour in the water, bring to the boil, turn down to a medium heat and cook for 15 minutes. Remove from the heat and leave to rest for 5 minutes.

4. Strain the pulp through a cheesecloth-lined sieve set over a large bowl. Leave for 2 hours to allow the juice to drip through. Don't be tempted to push the pulp though as this will just make the jelly cloudy.

5. Measure the strained liquid – you should have about 1.7 litres – pour it into the clean saucepan and place over a medium heat. Slowly add the sugar and bring to a rolling boil and cook for 20 minutes, or until the jelly reaches setting point, 105°C/220°F on a sugar thermometer. Pour into warm sterilised jars and seal immediately. Store in a cool dark place.

DAMSON & ANISE CHEESE SHAPES

Makes 6 x 100g moulds

Damsons are the tastiest little plums. I think we tend not to use them as much as other plums as they have a small stone and can be a little fiddly to prepare. If you can push through the initial preparation then the end result is a beautiful dark pink pulp that is excellent for baking with or using in jams and jellies. They are extremely high in pectin so they also make the best cheese (paste) that sets nicely. Try pouring it into moulds – I use metal ones with pretty textures that I've picked up at flea markets. Have fun with moulds of different shapes and sizes. Another idea is to set the cheese into a loaf tin and slice it.

1kg damsons
1 teaspoon ground star anise
150ml water
500g caster sugar
oil, for greasing

1. Put the damsons in a heavy-based saucepan with the star anise and water. Set over a medium heat and cook for 10 minutes or until the damsons are cooked all the way through and have softened. Remove from the heat and leave to cool for a few minutes. Pass the pulp through a mouli and discard the stones. Do be frugal and try not to waste any of the fruit pulp as you need as much of it as possible.

2. Put the fruit pulp in a clean saucepan with the sugar, set over a medium heat and stir until the sugar has dissolved. Turn the heat down to low and cook the paste gently for 1½ hours or until you can drag a wooden spoon across the paste and it leaves a line. The paste might start splattering like mini volcano tops so it's best to use a saucepan like a Le Creuset that has high sides.

3. Lightly oil your moulds. Pour the hot paste into the moulds and gently tap them on the work surface to release any air bubbles. Cover with parchment paper and leave overnight at room temperature to set. To release from the moulds, gently run a hot knife around the sides and slowly pull out.

PEAR & MARSALA JAM

Makes 8 x 220g jars

Pear jam is tricky because pears have so little pectin. For this recipe, I used Madernassa pears, which hail from the Roero region of northwest Italy. These rustic pears are traditionally used as a cooking pear because they hold their shape – do ensure they are super ripe, though. You can use any pear you like in this recipe provided they are very soft. If your pears are hard, leave them on a window ledge until they soften before making this jam.

2kg ripe pears, quartered, peeled and cored
600ml water
400ml Marsala wine
800g caster sugar
200g Green Apple Stock Jelly (see page 160)

1. Slice the pear quarters into chunky 1cm/½in cubes. Put them in a heavy-based saucepan with the water and Marsala and bring to the boil. Reduce the heat to a simmer and cook for 15 minutes or until the pears are super soft and about three-quarters of the liquid has evaporated. If the pears still feel firm towards the end of the cooking time, give them a gentle mash with a wooden spoon.

2. Slowly add the sugar and bring the jam back to the boil. Add the jelly and boil for about 15 minutes or until the jam reaches setting point, 105°C/220°F on a sugar thermometer; it will need a little longer than other jams. Remove from the heat and leave to rest for 5 minutes before pouring into warm sterilised jars and sealing immediately. Store in a cool dark place.

TIP
Replace the Marsala with water if you prefer and add a few
tablespoons of chopped candied ginger if you're feeling
more traditional.

CROWN PRINCE SQUASH JAM

Makes 2 x 750ml jars

I grew up eating pumpkins and only ever knew them as that until I moved to the UK and started eating squash. I am pretty sure they are exactly the same and just have different names on opposite sides of the world. When I think of pumpkins now I think of the gigantic orange ones purposely grown for carving at Halloween that are quite tasteless. Whereas squash are delicious roasting or steaming vegetables that come in all manner of crazy shapes and sizes. One of the more common autumn squash is the Crown Prince, which is perfect for cooking as it holds its shape and isn't watery. These qualities make it ideal for jam. This recipe has savoury notes that remind me of a red bean jam I once was given in Japan; the texture and flavour make it extremely moreish.

1 x 2kg Crown Prince squash (you should end up with 1kg flesh
   after it has been skinned and deseeded)
200ml water
1 vanilla pod, halved lengthways and the seeds
   scraped out and cook both into the jam
650g caster sugar
100g Green Apple Stock Jelly (see page 160)

1. Halve the squash and place each half, flesh-side down, on a board. Cut each half in half again and then cut off the skin. Scoop out the seeds and chop the flesh into 5cm/2in pieces. Put the squash in a steamer and cook until tender, about 25 minutes.

2. Put the cooked squash in a bowl to cool for 5 minutes or until you can handle it. I like to keep the pieces in rough shapes but you can choose whether to chop it up, purée it or keep it rough and ready. Put the squash in a heavy-based saucepan with the water, set over a medium heat and cook until the squash starts to break down. The water should stop it from catching in the pan.

3. Scrape the seeds from the vanilla pod and add the seeds and pod to the pan. Slowly add the sugar and jelly. Bring to the boil and cook for 10 minutes or until the jam reaches setting point, 105°C/220°F on a sugar thermometer. Pour into warm sterilised jars and seal immediately. I like to keep this in the fridge as I am constantly scooping jam out of the jar – it won't last.

TIP
Another similar squash variety is the Queensland Blue. Very generous in the garden and has a firm waxy texture, perfect for cooking into a jam.

FALLEN APPLE MALTED BUTTER
Makes 8 x 220g jars

The word 'butter' is fake advertising here as this isn't a creamy dairy fat that you would usually slather onto your toast but rather a smooth fruit spread that you would use instead of regular butter – unless you like butter with your apple. You can play around with the amount of sugar here, and if you want to use less then do. You will need to refrigerate the apple butter after it's cooled down as opposed to sealing it in a jar and storing it for a long time.

1.5kg apples (use a mix of whatever is available but try to ensure half are sour apples like cookers), peeled, cored and roughly chopped
500ml apple juice
400g light brown sugar
250g malted barley extract
1 teaspoon sea salt
juice of 1 lemon
1 vanilla pod, cut in half lengthways and seeds scraped out

1. Put the apples in a heavy-based saucepan with the apple juice, sugar, malted barley extract and salt. Set over a medium heat and cook for 20 minutes or until the apples are soft. Remove from the heat and leave to rest for 5 minutes. Use a handheld stick blender to blitz the mix until it is a smooth butter-like consistency.

2. Add the lemon juice and vanilla seeds and return the pan to a very low heat and cook for 1½ hours or until the mixture is thick enough to run a wooden spoon through it and leave a line. Be very careful when cooking this to keep the heat very low, and watch it doesn't catch. Alternatively, you can bake the purée in the oven at 130°C/250°F/gas mark 1 for 2 hours, stirring every 20 minutes or so to ensure it doesn't catch and the top doesn't become too dark.

3. Spoon into warm sterlisied jars and seal immediately. You can't pour this as it's too thick so it will need to be spooned in and then the jars tapped to release any air bubbles.

TIP
Cooking this pureé is very similar to making Damson & Anise Cheese Shapes (see page 140). It's cooked slow and low for a very long time. Be careful of the hot pockets of apple lava.

SLOE & CELERY LEAF GIN
Makes 1 x 2 litre bottles

Little hands are what you need here. Sloe bushes have large spikes and big hands can struggle getting to most of the little fruit, so if you have some small people around perhaps they can help you. Try to hold out until the first frost before picking your sloes as they will be much plumper and easier to pick, making your gin tipple much tastier. I usually start seeing sloes in early autumn and have learnt that they need much more time on the tree to develop. However, you need to be on standby to get them before other humans and birds beat you to it. I like to make this infused gin in a large jar and then decant it into small ones once it's ready. Leaving this for as long as possible is key, so you must try and get into the annual rhythm of making this drink and then you will have a year-round supply. I start by making this during autumn – it's ready by the following autumn, which is then time to harvest again, so once you have waited that initial year you should have enough to see you through until your next batch.

**650g sloes (prick each one to help the juice bleed into the gin or if they have
   been frozen they will burst upon defrosting which makes them split)**
½ cup celery leaves
400g caster sugar
750ml gin

1. Put the sloes into a sterilised 2-litre jar, followed by the celery leaves, then add the sugar and mix with your hand. Pour over the gin and then screw on the lid and leave for a week.

2. For the next month, whenever you can remember, give the jar a light shake to mix all the ingredients and help the sugar to dissolve. I like to leave the sloes in the gin for a full year and then strain it when it is ready to drink.

TIP
You could try making this with any small tart plums like damsons or wild bullace. Try not to use sweeter plums.

CHASSELAS GRAPE JAM

Makes 8 x 220g jars

Chasselas grapes are a common wine grape variety that are used to make a full, dry and fruity white wine. They are heavily seeded and carry high sugars and acidity, which makes them delicious as a table grape. They are also ideal for jam-making as they are plump and juicy, though you will need a little time on your hand (even more than for the Uva Fragola grapes, see page 113) as they don't peel as easily.

2kg Chasselas grapes
500g caster sugar
400g Green Apple Stock Jelly (see page 160) or any other jelly you can spare
juice of 1 lemon

1. Set yourself up with a large bowl for the peeled grapes and juices and another for the skins. Remove the grapes from the stalks. Individually peel the skins off each grape, working over a bowl so that you collect as much of the juice as possible. Put the peeled grapes in with the juice and the skins in the second bowl. If, like me, about three-quarters of the way through you become a little bored with peeling the grapes, you can add the rest of the unpeeled grapes to the peeled ones; this is cheating though. Weigh the grapes and juice. You should have about 1.5kg of grapes and juice and about 300g of skins. Set aside the skins in the second bowl.

2. Put the grapes and juices in a heavy-based saucepan and set over a medium heat. Cook for 10 minutes at a gentle simmer until they have softened.

3. Remove from the heat and pass the mixture through a mouli, the mouli will catch the seeds. You should end up with about 1kg of grapeflesh pulp.

4. Put the pulp and skins in a heavy-based saucepan, set over a medium heat and cook for 5 minutes or until the skins start breaking down. Slowly add the sugar, jelly and lemon juice and cook for a further 15 minutes or until the jam reaches setting point, 105°C/220°F on a sugar thermometer. Pour into warm sterilised jars and seal immediately. Store in a cool dark place..

TIP
Be aware that this is a soft set jam, even though you have added apple pectin stock.

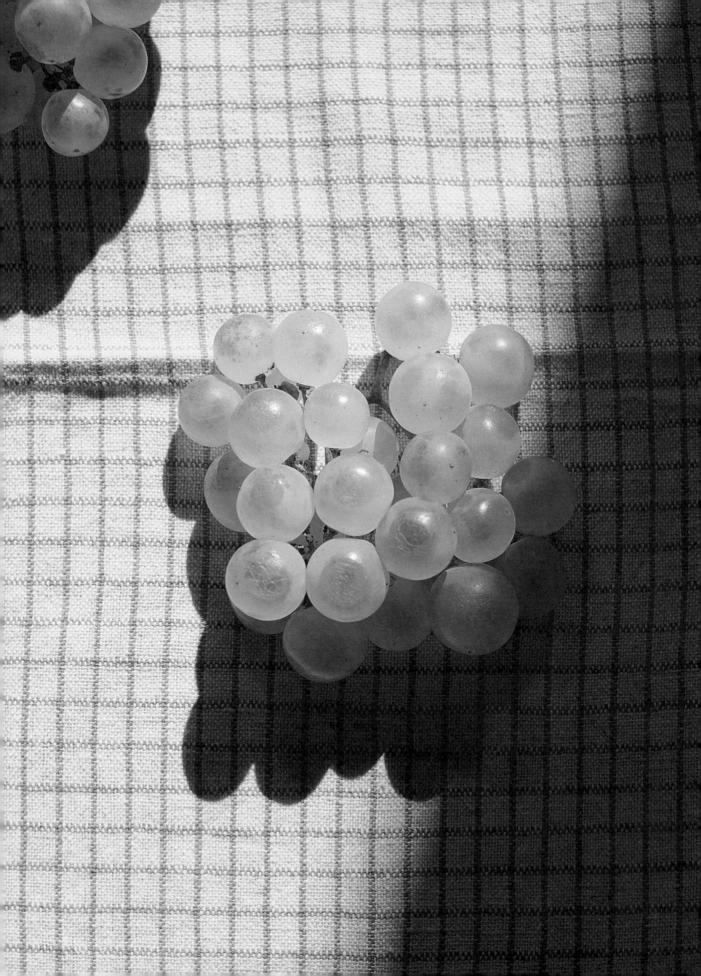

ACIDIC

DARK

COMFORTING

BITING

COSY

F R

YORKSHIRE
RHUBARB

Mid January is a time when the gloom of the winter begins setting in and I start feeling restless, trying to imagine what light and warmth feels like again. When I started working as a pastry chef at St. John Bread and Wine in 2008 I realised how much the seasons correlated with what ingredients we used. Yorkshire forced rhubarb was one of these.

Working with the seasons really excited me, and as I had just started my new role in the summer it meant an abundance of beautiful fruit to work with. Later in the year I would experience my first winter, and as January approached I was a little anxious for some vibrancy, colour and new ingredients. The first time I encountered Yorkshire forced rhubarb was on a typical grey January day. My eyes lit up in astonishment as I was presented with a box of this hot pink vegetable. I had never seen anything like it before; it was so bright and had an electric energy to it, fluorescent. I loved it instantly. It was so much sweeter and more delicate than outdoor-grown rhubarb. It became a sign of good things to come and it couldn't have been more of a contrasting seasonal colour to get the season started. For the next four years, the arrival of the first Yorkshire forced rhubarb heralded more exciting times in the pastry kitchen.

To celebrate this Frost chapter, I decided to go and visit a forced rhubarb producer and came upon Robert Tomlinson in Pudsey, West Yorkshire. I set off on a late Febuary afternoon in search of catching the vegetable at its peak and to find a farm that still honours such traditions, desperately hoping that I wouldn't miss it.

Robert and his family have a farm in the Yorkshire rhubarb triangle, which runs between Bradford, Leeds and Wakefield. The farm has been in the family for four generations and they are one of only two farms left in Pudsey, the other remaining eight are in Wakefield. They produce their rhubarb under the family name Tomlinsons and proudly display the Protected Designation of Origin (PDO) stamp on their packaging.

Pudsey used to have as many as 200 farms producing traditional forced rhubarb before the Second World War. Now what remains on Robert's farm is four sheds for growing the rhubarb indoors and large vacant plots outside, ready for growing the crowns.

'I hope little David one day decides to take on the Tomlinson legacy, producing the finest rhubarb in the triangle allowing us to keep enjoying this magical vegetable.'

The cycle begins...

Back in the 1970s, the Tomlinsons began to grow rhurbarb, with two varieties, Stockbridge Harbinger and Stockbridge Arrow, and only thirty crowns (roots) of each set. Today they have over 150,000 crowns, derived from years of splitting the original crowns, a process that takes place in October and early spring when the soil isn't too wet. Split crowns can produce up to six new ones. Once planted, the crowns remain in the ground for two years to allow the roots to establish themselves and become strong enough to be uprooted and taken into the dark sheds for forcing. There they are placed, not planted, in rows, on highly fertile soil and packed together like a jigsaw puzzle. The gaps are then filled with soil so that as the stalks grow they stand up neatly, supporting each other. The sheds are heated and kept dark for up to six weeks, conditions that force the plants to grow rapidly. Starved of light, photosynthesis cannot take place, which is why the stalks are so pink and the leaves yellow.

Forced rhubarb stalks are carefully picked by hand once they have reached the perfect size. Candles are placed along the rows so that the workers can see to pick. I have read many times that forced rhubarb is grown under candlelight, which isn't the case. It is grown in the dark and picked under the gentle light of candles so that it can be seen yet not affected by light.

After five to six weeks, the rhubarb crowns tire and the stalks grow thinner. Once they start going to seed, picking stops and Robert will open out the doors at both ends of the sheds to let the roots decompose and the tops turn to compost. Within four to five months, the entire plants – crowns and tops – will have turned into compost and will be removed and put back onto the land alongside shoddy, a natural soil fertiliser. Shoddy is the name for the multicoloured scraps of wool, collected traditionally from old mills, which would have been dotted around the rhubarb triangle. It's a great example of recycling a local product. Robert now collects his shoddy from Hainsworth Mill, which has been producing wool fabric for more than 225 years. He describes the mill as 'being on the go forever, just like us'. The compost and shoddy are used to prepare the ground for another season of planting crowns. The Yorkshire forced rhubarb season finishes in early April, just when the outdoor season begins.

This whole process takes just over two years, from planting the crown to harvesting those pretty in pink stalks. Spending some time with Robert and his son David made me feel so much more passionate about this traditional farming method, yet a little sad that it seems to be dying out in the UK. I hope Little David one day decides to take on the Tomlinson legacy, producing the finest rhubarb in the triangle, allowing us to keep enjoying this magical vegetable.

YORKSHIRE FORCED RHUBARB & GRAPPA JAM

Makes 5 x 220g jars

Out of respect for this very special vegetable, it is really important to make this jam in small batches, otherwise it ends up boiling for too long and you lose the vibrancy of both colour and flavour. As the Yorkshire forced rhubarb season comes to an end you will notice that a few boxes of seconds (thinner stalks) might start appearing in markets, which are a bit cheaper in price. These are the last of the stems that the crowns would have produced at the five to six weeks maturation and are perfect for jam-making. Try to select the pinkest ones possible so that the jam has a strong colour.

1kg forced rhubarb
600g caster sugar
juice of 1 lemon
100ml grappa (optional)

1. Trim the leaves from the rhubarb stalks and discard. Wash the stalks in cold water.

2. Slice the rhubarb into 2cm/¾in pieces and put in a heavy-based preserving pan. Set the pan over a medium heat and slowly cook the rhubarb until it starts to break down, being careful not to let it catch on the bottom of the pan.

3. Once it has started to soften, slowly add the sugar and lemon juice. Bring to the boil and boil for 8 minutes, stirring so that it doesn't catch, or until the jam reaches setting point, 105°C/220°F on sugar thermometer. You may need to turn the heat down a little if it does start to catch. Turn off the heat and leave the jam to rest for 5 minutes, stirring every minute to distribute the bubbles. Pour into warm sterilised jars and seal immediately. Store in a cool dry place.

'YUM.'

TIPS

As Yorkshire forced rhubarb has been awarded Protected Designation of Origin status, it will be hard to find outside the UK so perhaps try growing your own in a terracotta cloche in your garden, which provides the same forcing conditions.

Grappa is a spirit made in Italy from the skins left over from pressing grapes for wine. It is very high in alcohol – 40–60 per cent – and is traditionally served as a digestive after dinner.

GREEN APPLE STOCK JELLY

Makes 10 x 220g jars

This is a naturally set jelly that you can make with Bramley apples, though crab apples work equally as well. In the UK, Bramleys grow in abundance and are harvested in August/September. They are then kept in cold storage, which means they are available all year around. I make this jelly to help with the set when turning fruit that are low in pectin into jam. The idea is to make a plain jelly with a neutral flavour that can be kept refrigerated or sealed in jars and stored in your larder. Using a set jelly is far superior to using a liquid base apple stock that would dilute your jam and flavour.

2kg Bramley apples
3 litres cold water
1.5kg caster sugar
1 lemon

1. Wash the apples, cut into quarters and then halve these chunks again. Put the chunks in a heavy-based saucepan and pour over the water. Slowly bring to the boil and cook until the apples start to break down, about 30 minutes.

2. Remove from the heat and pass the pulp through a cheesecloth-lined sieve set over a large bowl. Leave for 2 hours to allow the juice to drip through. Don't push the apple pulp though the cloth or the liquid will become cloudy. It should produce about 1.7 litres of strained juice.

3. Pour the liquid into a clean saucepan, add the sugar and lemon juice and slowly bring to the boil. Once it is on a rolling boil, cook until the jam reaches setting point, about 15 minutes and 105°C/220°F on a sugar thermometer. Pour into warm sterilised jars and seal immediately. Store in a cool dark place.

TIPS

If you live in Australia or the US where Bramley apples are not grown, you can use Granny Smith apples, which are also high in pectin.

A couple of tablespoons of this jelly in a stew lifts the flavours. I use approx 200g of Green Apple Stock Jelly in my jam recipes if the fruit in the starring role is low in pectin, for example, cherries and pears.

SEVILLE ORANGE & CHAMOMILE MARMALADE
Makes 7 x 220g jars

This is my foolproof marmalade recipe. I cook the fruit whole, which makes it set more easily. If you are organised enough, cook the fruit the night before and leave to cool overnight – this makes the fruit easier to handle. It is really important to use Seville oranges, a variety of orange that is very high in pectin, and which also guarantees that traditional bitter marmalade flavour.

1kg unwaxed Seville oranges (about 8 oranges)
1.5 litres water
1.2kg caster sugar
20g dried chamomile flowers
juice of 1 lemon

1. Remove the stalk ends from the oranges and place them, whole, in a heavy-based saucepan with the water. Cover the pan with a lid and bring to the boil. Once it has started boiling, reduce the heat to a gentle simmer and cook for 30–35 minutes. Remove from the heat and leave to cool down completely.

2. Once cool, remove the whole oranges and put in a bowl. Strain the cooking liquid, reserving 1 litre. Transfer the reserved liquid to a bowl.

3. Halve all the oranges and scoop out the flesh over a sieve set over the reserved liquid. Once you have strained as much juice from the flesh as possible, discard the flesh.

4. Slice the orange rinds according to your preference and put into a clean preserving pan with the reserved liquid, sugar, chamomile flowers and lemon juice and bring to the boil. Boil for 20–25 minutes, until the marmalade reaches setting point, 105°C/220°F on a sugar thermometer. Remove from the heat and leave to rest for 10 minutes. Pour into warm sterilised jars and seal immediately. Store in a cool, dark place.

TIP
I like to play around with how I cut the peel, creating diamond shapes or slicing it paper-thin. You can be as creative here as you like.

CRANBERRY & SHERRY VINEGAR JAM

Makes 10 x 220g jars

This is the perfect jam to make for Christmas as it is really versatile; it goes with all your Christmas meats and cheeses, and you can also cheat and use this in your trifle to add some punch. I like to cook the cranberries slowly with the spices and citrus zest to give it more flavour. When you cook them they make a popping sound, which I always think means they are bursting with festive spirit! Try your local greengrocer for fresh cranberries, which are available in December in the UK. Frozen ones will work but this jam will always taste better made with fresh.

1kg cranberries
250ml water
1 cinnamon stick
zest and juice of 1 unwaxed orange, plus any leaves attached to the fruit (optional)
zest and juice of 1 unwaxed lemon, plus any leaves attached to the fruit (optional)
600g caster sugar
150ml sherry vinegar (look for the brand Valdespino)

1. Wash the cranberries in cold water and put in a heavy-based saucepan with the water, cinnamon stick, citrus zest and any citrus leaves, if using, and slowly bring to a simmer. Cook gently for 15 minutes, stirring carefully. The cranberries will start popping as they cook.

2. Once the fruit has broken down, slowly add the sugar, citrus juice and vinegar. Bring to the boil and boil rapidly for 15 minutes. If you feel the mixture is a bit thick, stir in a little extra water. (Cranberries are very high in pectin so if the jam doesn't have enough liquid it will set very firmly, which, to me, isn't very nice.) This is a jam that may catch so stay with it and stir occasionally to ensure it doesn't burn on the base of the pan.

3. Remove the cinnamon stick, pour into warm sterilised jars and seal immediately. Store in a cool dark place.

> TIP
> This jam works really well with a soft cows' milk cheese –
> I like Tunworth for its earthy, rich mushroom flavour.

CLEMENTINE & FINO JAM
'UPSIDE DOWN CHRISTMAS'
Makes 7 x 220g jars

Growing up in Australia and celebrating Christmas as part of the hot summer is the exact opposite of the British version. After twelve years in London, I've embraced the mistletoe, crackling log fires, warm panettone and bowls of leafy clementines.

1.5kg clementines or satsumas
juice of 2 lemons
650ml water
700g caster sugar
200g Green Apple Stock Jelly (see page 160)
100ml fino sherry

1. Wash and peel the clementines or satsumas, reserving the peel from four of them. Break up all the segments. Cut each segment in half vertically from top to bottom.

2. Slice the reserved peel into fine threads and put in a small saucepan and cover with 650ml water. Bring to the boil, then turn down to a simmer for 5 minutes.

3. Once the rind is soft, add it and the cooking liquid to a heavy-based saucepan with the segmented fruit, lemon juice, water, sugar and jelly and slowly bring to the boil. Cook for 30–35 minutes, or until the jam reaches setting point, 105°C/220°F on a sugar thermometer. Remove from the heat and carefully stir in the sherry – it will bubble and splatter. Leave to rest for 5 minutes before pouring into warm sterilised jars, sealing immediately. Store in a cool dark place.

TIP
Slightly warm this jam and serve it with your Christmas pudding alongside brandy butter or enjoy on toasted panettone.

PINK GRAPEFRUIT & SMOKED SALT MARMALADE

Makes 7 x 220g jars

I have a fond memory of grapefruit from my childhood, remembering my uncle eating half a grapefruit at the breakfast table, sprinkling it with salt and scooping the flesh out generously with a spoon. This salty/sharp flavour pairing seems to be common at my local Turkish greengrocer, too, where they dip tiny green sour plums into salt. I thought it was perfect to add a little salt to this sweet, sour and acidic citrus fruit.

1.5kg pink grapefruits (about 5 grapefruits)
2 litres water
juice of 2 lemons
1.2kg caster sugar
1 teaspoon smoked salt

1. Lightly wash the grapefruits and remove the stalk ends. Halve and squeeze the juice into a bowl. Set the juice aside.

2. Scoop out as much of the pith from the rinds as you can and set aside. Cut each half rind in half again. Place the pith and any seeds on a square of cheesecloth and tie up tightly.

3. Slice the rind of four of the grapefruits to your desired thickness – I prefer to slice it thinly as the rind is so bitter and this is a delicate marmalade. Discard the rind of the remaining grapefruit, put the sliced rind and water into a heavy-based saucepan and bring to the boil, then reduce the heat to a gentle simmer and cook for 30 minutes or until the rind is cooked and soft.

4. Add the grapefruit juice, lemon juice, sugar and salt and bring back to the boil. Boil rapidly for 45 minutes or until the marmalade reaches setting point, 105°C/220°F on a sugar thermometer. Remove from the heat and leave to rest for 10 minutes. Pour into warm sterilised jars and seal immediately. Store in a cool dark place. This marmalade will last for six months.

TIPS
Pink grapefruit, once called 'forbidden fruit', was
an accidental cross between a pomelo and a
sweet orange.

These bitter grapefruits are also delicious dehydrated
(see the recipe for Dehydrated Blood Orange Discs, on
page 178). As I am not a huge fan of eating them fresh,
I love them dried and crumbled over my porridge,
the texture helping to steer my palate away from
the bitterness.

LEAFY LEMON & VANILLA MARMALADE

Makes about 8 x 220g jars

I always try and find the finest Amalfi lemons for this recipe as they are unwaxed, have a fragrant, thicker rind and taste less acidic than most lemons. If you can't find ones from Italy's Amalfi coast then any unwaxed lemon will work – Spain also produces really lovely lemons. Lemons are generally given a coat of wax to help extend their shelf life. I try and buy unwaxed ones as the wax makes them harder to slice and zest. If you're buying unwaxed lemons then keep them in the fridge to extend their shelf life. You could also tear up the leaves and steep them into sugar for a few weeks to draw out the natural oil and flavour, then use the sugar in baking.

800g leafy unwaxed Italian lemons
    (reserve the leaves – see tip)
1.15 litres water
700g caster sugar
1 vanilla pod, halved lengthways and the seeds
    scraped out and cook both into the jam
pinch of sea salt

1. Wash and dry the lemons and trim the stem ends. Cut in half vertically and try to remove as many seeds as possible. Wrap the seeds in cheesecloth and tie with some string and set aside.

2. Slice the lemons horizontally to your desired thickness, then put in a heavy-based preserving pan and cover with the water. Bring to the boil and then reduce the heat to a gentle simmer for 10 minutes or until the peel is soft to the touch.

3. Add the sugar, vanilla, cheesecloth-wrapped seeds and salt to the pan. Slowly bring to the boil and boil rapidly for 12 minutes or until setting point is reached, 85°C/185°F on a sugar thermometer.

4. Remove from the heat and rest for 5 minutes. Pour into warm sterilised jars and seal immediately. This marmalade sets very easily due to the high acid content from the citrus and the sugar. Store in a cool dark place.

BERGAMOT MARMALADE

Makes 10 x 220g jars

Bergamot citrus fruit can be slightly harder to find than your average lemons and limes, but they are worth the hunt as their natural scent, which is used to flavour Earl Grey tea, is really beautiful and so different from any other citrus you will find. Traditionally bergamots were harvested for their strong-scented oil and used in the perfume industry. If you find this marmalade is too scented for your liking, try using half lemons and half bergamots to mellow out the flavour. Bergamot is a bitter citrus fruit that produces an intense marmalade, not for the faint hearted. I use the fruit whole, which creates a firm set, perfect for spreading on toasted panettone. If you prefer lighter-tasting marmalades try my Leafy Lemon & Vanilla Marmalade.

1.5kg bergamots
juice of 2 lemons
1.2kg caster sugar
1.5 litres water
pinch of sea salt

1. Wash and dry the bergamots and trim off the ends and stalk ends. Cut in half vertically and try to remove as many seeds as possible. Wrap the seeds in cheesecloth and tie with some string and set aside.

2. Cut each bergamot half into quarters and then into fine slices (it's best if they are not too big and chunky). Put them in a heavy-based preserving pan and cover with cold water. Bring to the boil and reduce the heat to a gentle simmer for 15 minutes.

3. Once the rind is soft, strain the slices, discarding the water. Put the strained slices in a cleaned saucepan with the lemon juice, sugar, cheesecloth-wrapped seeds, salt and water and bring to the boil. Boil rapidly for 40 minutes or until the marmalade reaches setting point, 105°C/220°F on a sugar thermometer. Remove from the heat and leave to rest for 10 minutes. Pour into warm sterilised jars and seal immediately. Store in a cool dark place.

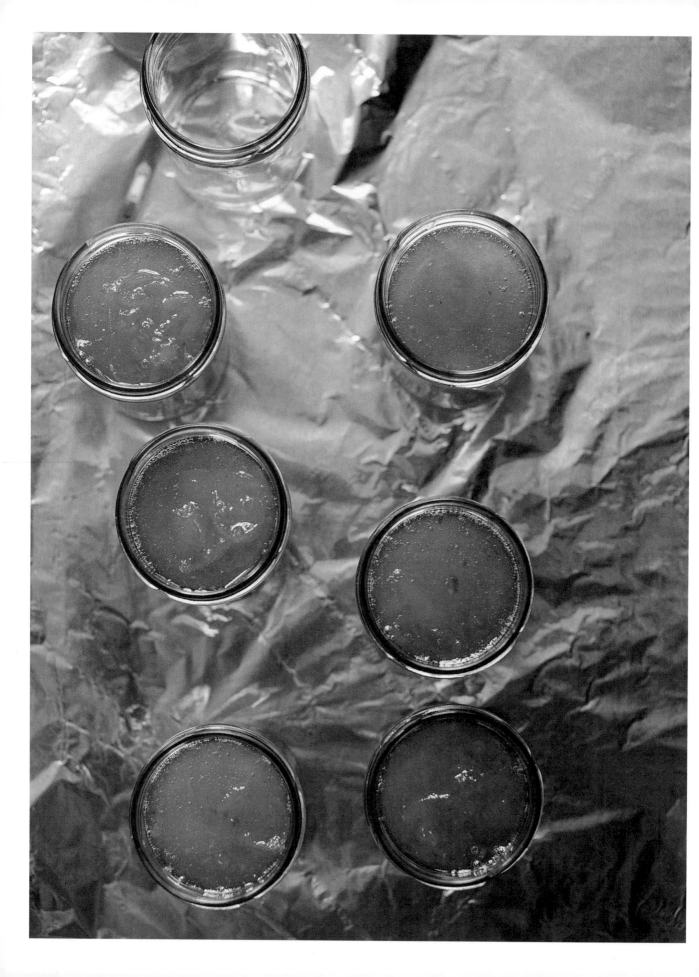

KUMQUAT & BRANDY MARMALADE

Makes 5 x 220g jars

Most of the people I know who have kumquat trees grow them in pots as ornamentals and find themselves with an excess of these tiny citrus fruit. Kumquats have sweet peel and tangy flesh, which means they are perfect for making a marmalade that, unlike the classic Seville orange, isn't at all bitter. The combination of kumquat and brandy makes a really rich, silky marmalade. If you manage to find a kumquat tree, then pick some of the leaves as you can add these to the recipe for extra earthy flavour.

1kg kumquats, plus a few leaves if you have any
1.5 litres water
700g caster sugar
juice of 1 lemon
100ml brandy

1. Wash the kumquats and cut into 2mm slices. Put them in a heavy-based saucepan and add the water and any fresh kumquat leaves. Set over a low heat and gently bring to the boil, reduce the heat and simmer for 15 minutes or until the kumquats are tender.

2. Slowly add the sugar and lemon juice and boil for 15 minutes or until the marmalade reaches setting point, 105°C/220°F on a sugar thermometer.

3. Remove from the heat and leave to rest for 5 minutes, then stir in the brandy. Pour into warm sterilised jars and seal immediately. Store in a cool dark place. The marmalade will last for six months.

SALTED MANDARINS & PINK PEPPERCORNS
Makes 1 x 1kg jar

I have chosen to preserve mandarins instead of lemons, which are the most commonly preserved citrus fruit, especially in the Middle East. I thought it would be nice to salt mandarins whole, including the fruit inside and their thin rind, so that you could use the entire fruit instead of just using the skin as you do with preserved lemons. The sweet mandarin adds a depth to slow braises and tagines.

1kg mandarins
500g coarse rock salt
5 fresh bay leaves
2 teaspoons pink peppercorns
500g mandarin juice

1. Quarter the mandarins with a sharp knife but do not cut through the whole fruit as you want to keep the bases intact. Place them in a bowl and add the salt, bay leaves and peppercorns.

2. Carefully mix the ingredients together and push the salt into the insides of the fruit. Place them, whole, in a sterilised jar with the bay leaves and peppercorns.

3. Pour in the mandarin juice. If you don't have enough liquid to cover the fruit, top up with water. Seal and leave for two months before using.

TIPS
Try salting other citrus fruit, such as navel oranges, grapefruits, bergamots, blood oranges or cedro lemons and try different herbs and spices to flavour them.

Add a small handful of thinly sliced salted clementine rind halfway through roasting waxy potatoes. The salted rind will become deliciously caramelised. Once cooked, add baby capers and chopped parsley.

APPLE & ROSÉ WINE JELLY

Makes 5 x 220g jars

This is an old classic that my mum used to make, adapted from a 1970s recipe. Instead of using Bramley apples, the classic English cooking apple, it calls for Granny Smiths, which are a little sweeter, though still tart enough. I like the flavour that comes from using a rosé wine but I think a white wine such as Riesling would work just as well.

1.2kg Granny Smith apples
1 unwaxed lemon
1.8 litres water
270ml rosé wine
1.2kg caster sugar

1. Wash the fruit and slice the unpeeled apples and lemon into quarters, then slice each one in half. Put in a heavy-based saucepan with the water and bring to the boil. Reduce the heat to a simmer and cook, covered, for 45 minutes.

2. Add the wine, cover the pan with a lid and simmer for a further 20 minutes. (Keeping the lid on means the alcohol won't evaporate.)

3. Strain the mixture through cheesecloth suspended over a bowl overnight. Don't squeeze the bag as it will make the jelly cloudy.

4. The following day, discard the pulp (put in your compost) and measure the strained liquid. You should end up with approx. 1.3 litres of liquid.

5. Pour the liquid into a preserving pan, add the sugar and slowly bring to the boil. Boil rapidly for 10–15 minutes, until the jelly reaches setting point, 105°C/220°F on a sugar thermometer. Pour into warm sterilised jars and seal immediately. Store in a cool dark place.

TIP
Play around with adding any leftover alcohol you may have hanging around. You could try a herby vermouth, which would pair perfectly with the tart apples and sugar.

OUTDOOR-GROWN RHUBARB & GREEN CARDAMOM JAM

Makes 10 x 220g jars

The sign that the short forced rhubarb season has come to an end is the first sightings of outdoor-grown rhubarb. This is usually around late March when the dormant perennial rhubarb begins to grow again. I think this is one of easiest vegetables to grow in the garden as it comes back every year and needs little help.

1.2kg outdoor-grown rhubarb
800g caster sugar
60ml water
2 tablespoons green cardamom pods
juice of 1 lemon

1. Toast the cardamom pods in a small frying pan set over a medium heat until they start to pop and turn light brown. Be careful as they can be quite lively! Remove from the heat and leave to cool.

2. Once cool, grind the pods using a electric spice grinder or pestle and mortar until the seeds inside are ground. (If using a pestle and mortar, you will need to sieve out the pods as they won't break down with the pestle.)

3. Mix the ground cardamom with sugar and leave for 24 hours to infuse the sugar.

4. When you are ready to make the preserve, wash the rhubarb and chop roughly into 5cm/2in pieces. Put in a heavy-based saucepan with the water and set over a medium heat. Once the rhubarb has started to break down, about 5 minutes, slowly add the sugar and lemon juice. Stir to combine.

5. Bring to the boil and cook until the jam reaches setting point, 105°C/220°F on a sugar thermometer. Remove from the heat and leave to rest for 5 minutes, stirring to distribute any bubbles, which will slowly disappear. Pour into warm sterilised jars and seal immediately. Store in a cool dark place.

DEHYDRATED BLOOD ORANGE DISCS

Makes 1 x 1-litre jar

Mid-winter heralds the citrus season and up until March we have a full range of blood oranges. Some are more intense that others, especially the Moro. I like to look out for varieties from Sicily, which are higher in quality and tend to have a dark blush colour – perfect for these dried discs. After spending most of winter with apples and chocolate, these blood oranges (alongside Yorkshire forced rhubarb) are a welcome sight. Ideally you will need a dehydrator. I use a small electric dehydrator at home, which is perfect for drying small batches of fruit, vegetables, herbs and flowers. If you have more space outdoors and are handy with a power drill you could build your own out of wood, which, visually, is much more appealing. You can also use a conventional oven but you will need to be careful as some ovens have irregular heat distribution and the discs may end up browning or burning very quickly.

5 blood oranges, preferably the Moro variety

1. Using a sharp knife, slice the oranges into thin round discs around 2–3mm (⅛in) thick and remove any seeds. Try not to make the slices too thin as they will become really brittle and lose their texture.

2. Place the slices in a single layer on the trays in your dehydrator and follow the manufacturer's instructions. Alternatively, drying in the oven is really easy, you just need to be able to set it on the lowest setting possible, around 140°C/275°F/ gas mark 1 or as low as you can go. Anything over 200°C/400°F/gas mark 6 will be too hot. Make a solution of water and lemon juice (250ml water, juice of 2 lemons) and dip the fruit segments in it before placing on a roasting tray to stop it from discolouring. Turn the fruit occasionally, making sure it doesn't stick and dries evenly. Once the oranges are completely dried, store in an airtight jar. They will last up to six months.

TIPS
Break up the discs and scatter through your granola or as a topping for your breakfast yogurt.

Blitz to a powder in a blender and use to marinate fish, meat and vegetables or dust salads with it.

PERSIMMON, SAFFRON & VANILLA JAM

Makes 7 x 220g jars

Persimmons or sharon fruit are known as *kaki* in Japan. They resemble tomatoes and have a sweet, honeyed flavour. There are two types of persimmons and I look out for the ones that resemble a flat peach or tomato as they are the astringent type that turn nicely into sweet ripe fruit. It's really important to select very ripe persimmons, that have a gooey jelly texture – perfect for jam-making – unlike the unripe fruit, which is not only hard but very bitter and sour.

1.5kg ripe persimmons
about 10 saffron threads
1 vanilla pod, cut in half lengthways and seeds scrapped out
800g unrefined caster sugar
juice of 1 lemon

1. Lightly wash the persimmons and remove the green tops. Slice the fruit into quarters and put in a preserving pan set over a low heat. Cook for about 10 minutes or until the fruit starts to slowly break down. Add the saffron and vanilla seeds. (You can also add the whole pod to the pan but remember to remove it later).

2. Continue to gently cook the jam for a further 5 minutes, so that the fruit has released more liquid, then slowly add the sugar and lemon juice. Bring to the boil and boil for about 10 minutes or until the jam reaches setting point, 105°C/220°F on a sugar thermometer. Remove from the heat and leaves to rest for 5 minutes. Pour into warm sterilised jars and seal immediately. Store in a cool dark place.

TIPS
You could also try roasting soft ripe persimmoms with sugar, verjuice and vanilla for a wintery dessert.

Serve the jam alongside a sharp sheep's milk yogurt and roasted pistachios.

CANDIED CEDRO
'CRAZY RIND'

Makes 1 x 1 litre jar

Cedro lemon (*Citrus medica*) is a rind-heavy citrus fruit that is prized for being highly scented. Also known as a citron, it is perfect for slowly cooking with sugar until it becomes transparent and sweet. You might find it difficult to find this fruit but good greengrocers should be able to help you, otherwise try a wholesale fruit or vegetable market. You won't mistake a cedro as they are very large in size, you may even come across varieties known as Buddha's Hand or Ponzino, which are both crazy-shaped, rind-heavy lemons, and also perfect for candying. You can also slice cedro thinly on a mandolin (being extremely careful) and serve fresh with extra virgin olive oil, flat-leaf parsley and salt and pepper as a side salad.

2 cedro lemons (around 800g)
1.5 litres water
500g caster sugar

1. Cut the cedros in half and then into quarters. Discard any flesh – there won't be much.

2. Cut the rind into 2cm/¾in cubes and put in a saucepan with 1 litre of water. Set over a medium heat, bring to the boil and then simmer for 40–45 minutes, until the rind is soft. Strain and discard the cooking water.

3. Put the sugar and remaining water into a clean saucepan and bring to the boil. Once the sugar has dissolved, add the cedro rind.

4. Cook over a medium heat for 30–40 minutes, until most of the water has evaporated and you are left with a thick syrup. Pour into a warm sterilised jar and keep in the fridge and use as needed. You can also strain the cedro cubes from the syrup, roll in caster sugar and leave on a wire rack for 24 hours to dry out.

> TIPS
> Use dehydrated citrus leaf powder in the sugar that you use to coat the cubes.
>
> Traditionally, in Italy, candied fruit are sometimes flavoured with mustard seeds and served with savoury dishes like *bolito misto*, which is a rich poached meat dish. The sweetness from candied fruit helps cut through the richness.
>
> Decorate the tops of your cakes with a little candied cedro.

APPLE CIDER &
CALVADOS JAM

Makes 9 x 220g jars

I am always trying to work out ways to use apples, but there are only so many ways to preserve them. It is more common to make a jelly with apples, so I set myself the task of making a jam with them; a recipe that I could use to cook the bags of apples my neighbours leave at the front of their house (yes I live in a city). You can play around with the apples you use, but I like Bramleys as they are sour and work perfectly with sugar. I often think of this as a compote jam as it's perfect added to a bowl of warming porridge.

1.3kg Bramley apples
750ml cider (preferably dry, such as a Breton cider)
700g caster sugar
juice of 1 lemon
80ml Calvados

1. Peel, quarter and core the apples. Cut the quarters in half and place in a heavy-based saucepan with the cider. Cook, covered with a lid, over a low heat for 10 minutes – you don't want to cook it over a high heat otherwise the cider completely evaporates.

2. Slowly add the sugar, lemon juice and Calvados, bring to the boil and cook for a further 10 minutes. Leave to rest for 5 minutes to disperse the bubbles. Pour into warm sterlisied jars and seal immediately. Store in a cool dark place.

MEDJOOL DATE &
CHESTNUT JAM

Makes approx. 6 x 220 jars

This is a very sweet jam as the dates contain natural sugar. Look out for chestnuts that feel heavy and keep them in a cool dark place to stop them from drying out.

700g fresh chestnuts
350g fresh Medjool dates, stoned
800g caster sugar
1 vanilla pod, halved lengthways and the seeds
    scraped out and cook both into the jam
juice of ½ lemon

1. To prepare the chestnuts, cut a cross in each one, add them to a saucepan of boiling water and blanch for 10 minutes. Strain the chestnuts into a sieve and leave for 5 minutes to cool, then peel and discard the brown papery skins.

2. Put the dates in a heavy-based saucepan with the peeled chestnuts. Cover with cold water, bring to the boil and simmer for 20 minutes or until the chestnuts are cooked. They should have the consistency of cooked potatoes, which you can test with the tip of a knife. You may need to reduce the heat down a little if you feel the water is evaporating too quickly.

3. Remove from the heat and rest for a few minutes, then whizz in a blender or put through a mouli until the mixture forms a thick paste. You should have about 1.3kg of purée.

4. Put the purée in a clean saucepan with the sugar and vanilla and cook over a low heat until the sugar has dissolved, then add the lemon juice and orange blossom water. Bring to the boil and cook for 15 minutes. Be careful as the hot mixture can spit and burn your arms. Keep stirring to make sure it doesn't catch, and if it does, turn down the heat a little. Pour into sterilised jars and seal immediately. With thick jam like this you will need to tap the jars on the worktop to get air bubbles out.

TIPS
Spread Medjool Date & Chestnut Jam over the middle layers of a Victoria Sponge or chocolate cake.

Use as a quick dessert option. Dollop over ice cream and sprinkle with pistachios. You may need to thin out the jam with a little water to make it softer in texture.

CHOCOLATE-DIPPED ORANGE PEEL
Makes 500g

These are perfect treats to eat when you have had your fill of festive meals and just want something small and sweet. They are also a nice little gift. They take time to make but it's worth it.

4 large unwaxed oranges
400g granulated sugar (use caster if you want a smooth appearance)
400ml water
200g dark chocolate, for coating

1. Cut the oranges in halves then into quarters. Cut each quarter in half again – this makes it easier to cut out the pith and the fruit segments. I like to use a flexible knife here as it will keep the rind even. Discard the pith but keep the fruit for another use. Cut each piece of peel into two on an angle. Put the peel in a saucepan and cover with water. Bring to the boil, then simmer gently for 10–12 minutes until the peel is cooked soft but still has some firmness. Be careful not to overcook these delicate pieces.

2. Once cooked, strain the peel and leave to rest. If you are intending to use the saucepan again, wash it thoroughly so that it doesn't have any impurities left from the orange peel, which would make the sugar syrup crystalize.

3. Put the sugar and water in a clean saucepan and bring to the boil. Reduce the heat to a simmer and add the cooked peel. Cook for 15 minutes over a medium heat and then turn off the heat and leave the peel to cool in the syrup.

4. Once cool, take the peel out of the syrup and gently roll each piece in sugar and place on a wire rack to dry out for 12 hours or overnight.

5. The next day, break the chocolate into pieces and put in a heatproof bowl set over a pan of barely simmering water, ensuring the bowl is not in contact with the water. Reduce the heat to a simmer and gently melt the chocolate, stirring constantly. Once the chocolate has melted, remove from the heat and leave to rest for 10 minutes with the bowl still on top of the saucepan. Dip each dried orange segment into the chocolate and place on baking parchment to set.

TIP
Why not grind up some roasted cardamom seeds to a fine powder or grind Dehydrated Blood Orange Discs (see page 178) to a powder and mix through your sugar before dusting and drying the orange peel.

Weight conversion chart

5g – ¹/₈ oz
10g – ¹/₄ oz
20g – ³/₄ oz
45g – 1 ²/₃ oz
50g – 1 ³/₄ oz
60g – 2 ¹/₄ oz
80g – 2 ³/₄ oz
85g – 3 oz
100g – 3 ¹/₂ oz
120g – 4 ¹/₄ oz
125g – 4 ¹/₂ oz
150g – 5 ¹/₂ oz
200g – 7 oz
220g – 8 oz
250g – 9 oz
300g – 10 ¹/₂ oz
350g – 12 oz
400g – 14 oz
500g – 1 lb 2 oz
550g – 1 lb 4 oz
600g – 1 lb 5 oz
650g – 1 lb 7 oz
700g – 1 lb 9 oz
750g – 1 lb 10 oz
800g – 1 lb 12 oz
900g – 2 lb
1kg – 2 lb 4 oz
1.1kg – 2 lb 8 oz
1.2kg – 2 lb 11 oz
1.25kg – 2 lb 12 oz
1.3kg – 2 lb 13 oz
1.4kg – 3 lb 2 oz
1.5kg – 3 lb 5 oz
1.6kg – 3 lb 8 oz
1.7kg – 3 lb 11 oz
1.8kg – 4 lb
1.9kg – 4 lb 4 oz
2kg – 4 lb 8 oz

Volume conversion chart

50ml – 2 fl oz
60ml – 4 tbsp
80ml – 5 ¹/₂ tbsp
100ml – 3 ¹/₂ fl oz
125ml – 4 fl oz
150ml – 5 fl oz / ¹/₄ pint
180ml – 6 fl oz
200ml – 7 fl oz / ¹/₃ pint
250ml – 9 fl oz
300ml – 10 fl oz / ¹/₂ pint
350ml – 12 fl oz
400ml – 14 fl oz
450ml – 16 fl oz
500ml – 18 fl oz
550ml – 19 fl oz
600ml – 20 fl oz / 1 pint
700ml – 1 ¹/₄ pints
750ml – 1 ¹/₃ pints
800ml – 27 fl oz
900ml – 1 ¹/₂ pints
1 litre – 1 ³/₄ pints
1.5 litres – 2 ²/₃ pints
1.8 litres – 3 pints
2.2 litres – 3 ³/₄ pints
2.5 litres – 4 ¹/₂ pints
3 litres – 5 ¹/₄ pints
3.3 litres – 5 ³/₄ pints
3.5 litres – 6 pints
5 litres – 8 ³/₄ pints
10 litres – 17 ¹/₂ pints

ACKNOWLEDGEMENTS & THANK YOU'S

Marcus Haslam, Mum and Dad, Jesse O'Brien, Alexandra Haynes, Janet Haynes, Mark Haynes, Daniel Haynes, Peter Haynes, Mary Indermaur, Charlotte Denniston, Marie-Claire Bridges, Dan Delaney, Robert Lowe, Noriko Miura, James Ferguson, Alethea Palmer, Maud Goodhart, Lauren Macdonald, Kitty Tench, Leila McAlister, Zoe Ross, Elena Heatherwick, Sophie Allen, Alix McAlister, Kyle Cathie, Judith Hannam, Naomi Masuda, Satoru Masuda, Justin Gellatly, Kenta Ohki, James Lowe, Fergus Henderson, Margot Henderson, Kaori Okuda, Paddy Plunkett, Natoora, Violet Cakes, Meral Karakas, Seref Aydin, Chatsworth Fruit and Veg, Mud Australia, Virginia Redmond, Barbara Dight, Square Root Soda Works, Ed Taylor, Robyn Simms, General Store Peckham, Ewald Damen, Anna-Marie Crowhurst, Tom Tivnan, Tom Macfarlane, Nicklas de León Persson, Andie Cusick, St. John Restaurant, Evie Saffron Strands, Jessica Koslow, Toru Saito, Maico Horiguchi, Chatsworth Road Market, Damian Patchell, European Salad Company, Tess Knowles, Sharon Dusic, Johnny Liu, Merlin Jones, Genevieve Schiffenhaus, Anna Jones, my LBJ shop regulars and all the LBJ wholesale customers for your continual support.